Simply COLORADO

Nutritious Recipes for Busy People

Colorado Dietetic Association

Published by:
Simply Colorado, Inc.
a subsidiary of Colorado Dietetic Association
4945 Meade Street
Denver, Colorado 80221

ISBN: 0–9626337–1–2

Printed by Eastwood Printing, Denver, Colorado

Introduction

From the great plains to snow–capped peaks to desert buttes to crystalline alpine lakes, Colorado's rich geography is as unique as our lifestyles. But no matter how diverse our lifestyles, we Coloradans have one thing in common — we want it all! Good health, good taste and good food are priorities, but most of us are too busy to cook. That's why the state's leading association for nutrition professionals, the Colorado Dietetic Association, developed *Simply Colorado — Nutritious Recipes for Busy People.*

Simply Colorado contains Colorado cuisine which is not only wholesome and nutritious but flavorful and easy to prepare. Each recipe is designed to fit into a healthful eating style. While preserving flavor and convenience, these recipes have been adapted to be lower in fat, cholesterol and sodium, and higher in fiber than traditional dishes.

The tempting offerings found in *Simply Colorado* have been developed and tested by Colorado's nutrition experts — Registered Dietitians who are members of the Colorado Dietetic Association. When you're seeking nutrition information or advice, be sure to look for the initials "RD" — Registered Dietitian. This credential is your assurance that a nutritionist has at least a baccalaureate degree in nutrition, dietetics or a closely related area from an accredited college or university; has completed a pre–professional supervised work experience; has passed an national qualifying exam; and participates in continuing education.

Simply Colorado acknowledges that people want delicious food but don't want to spend hours in the kitchen making it. Each recipe includes estimates of preparation and cooking time as well as nutrition information.

We dedicate *Simply Colorado* to all of you who, along with a busy and active lifestyle, value great health and great food!

Acknowledgements

First Edition

Cookbook Steering Committee

Kay Petre Massey, M.A., R.D., Chairman
Connie Auran, M.A., R.D.
Karen Christensen, M.S., R.D.
Patricia Daniluk, M.S., R.D.
Sara Lemley, M.P.H., R.D.

Editor — Kay Petre Massey, M.A., R.D.

Graphic Artist — Jennifer Collins

Word Processing — Louise Moore

Nutrition Analysis — Karen Christensen, M.S., R.D.
Practorcare Systems

Second Edition

Cookbook Steering Committee

Kay Petre Massey, M.A., R.D., Chairman
Helen A. Dorrough, M.S., R.D.
Lou Ann Dixon, M. Ed., R.D.
Clare Cusumano, R.D.
Pamela Ham, R.D.
Janet Franz

Editor — Kay Petre Massey, M.A., R.D.

Graphic Artist — Amy Mathiesen

Graphic Design — Louise Moore

Nutrition Analysis — Karen Christensen, M.S., R.D.
Practorcare Systems

Using the Nutrition Information

Each *Simply Colorado* recipe has been selected because it is lower in fat, cholesterol and sodium, and higher in fiber than its traditional counterpart. While representing healthful cuisine, these recipes are not intended for any specific dietary restriction and should not replace the advice of your physician or Registered Dietitian.

Major health organizations agree, a leading dietary concern is that Americans consume too much fat in their diet. This has spurred recommendations that for good health, fat intake should be limited to no more than 30 percent or less of total calories per day. This goal for fat intake is achieved most practically by finding a healthy balance between low–fat and high–fat foods.

The best way to keep your fat consumption balanced to reflect the 30 percent of calories from fat recommendation is to "budget" it. Everyone has a fat budget... the amount of fat you can reasonably eat each day. This fat "budget" depends on the total amount of calories you require each day. For this reason, men and active individuals can "afford" more fat than women and sedentary adults.

The following chart will help you identify your own personal "fat budget." As you work to stay within your "budget" each day, remember to eat a wide variety of foods in moderation. Rather than judging a food as "good" or "bad" based on fat content, match your favorite high–fat food with lean accompaniment throughout the day and stay within your "fat budget."

Your Fat Budget	If your daily calories are...	Your Fat Budget is...
	1,200 calories	44 grams or less
	1,500 calories	55 grams or less
	1,800 calories	66 grams or less
	2,100 calories	77 grams or less
	2,400 calories	88 grams or less
	2,700 calories	99 grams or less

Nutrient Analysis   Each *Simply Colorado* recipe has been analyzed for its nutrient content by the Practorcare Systems software program. We have provided information about each recipe's calorie, fat, cholesterol and sodium content to guide you in your use of the cookbook. While fiber is an important dietary consideration, accurate data on fiber in foods is currently unavailable and could not be included in our analysis.

Food Guide Pyramid
A Guide to Daily Food Choices

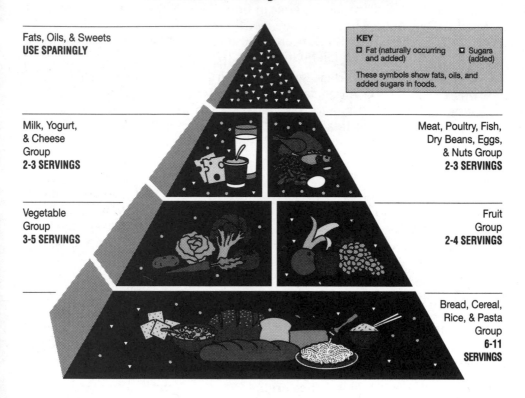

Fats, Oils, & Sweets
USE SPARINGLY

KEY
□ Fat (naturally occurring and added)   ◙ Sugars (added)
These symbols show fats, oils, and added sugars in foods.

Milk, Yogurt, & Cheese Group
2-3 SERVINGS

Meat, Poultry, Fish, Dry Beans, Eggs, & Nuts Group
2-3 SERVINGS

Vegetable Group
3-5 SERVINGS

Fruit Group
2-4 SERVINGS

Bread, Cereal, Rice, & Pasta Group
6-11 SERVINGS

The Colorado Dietetic Association encourages you to follow the USDA's *Food Guide Pyramid* as a guideline for evaluating your food intake. The Pyramid is based on research regarding what foods Americans eat, what nutrients are in these foods, and how to make the best food choices for you.

The Pyramid will help you choose what and how much to eat from each food group to get the nutrients you need without consuming too many calories, or too much fat, saturated fat, cholesterol, sugar, sodium or alcohol. Keep in mind these recommendations are for healthy Americans 2 years of age or more.

The Pyramid is an outline of what to eat each day. It's not a rigid pre-scription, but a general guide that lets you choose a healthful diet that's right for you.

What Counts as a Serving?

Bread, Cereal, Rice and Pasta

1 slice of bread   1 ounce of ready–to–eat cereal   1/2 cup of cooked cereal rice or pasta

Vegetables

1 cup of raw leafy vegetables   1/2 cup of other vegetables, cooked   3/4 cup of vegetable juice

Fruit

1 medium apple, banana, orange   1/2 cup of chopped, cooked or canned fruit   3/4 cup of fruit juice

Milk, Yogurt and Cheese

1 cup of milk or yogurt $1\frac{1}{2}$ ounces of natural cheese   2 ounces of process cheese

Meat, Poultry, Fish, Dry Beans, Eggs and Nuts

2–3 ounces of cooked lean meat, poultry or fish   1/2 cup of cooked dry beans, 1 egg or 2 tablespoons of peanut butter count as 1 ounce of lean meat

Modifying Your Favorite Recipes

Eating healthy doesn't mean giving up all of your favorite recipes. By modifying your recipes to include lower–fat ingredients and lower–fat cooking methods, many will easily fit healthful eating. To get started, ask the following questions about your recipe:

1. Do any of the ingredients come in a low–fat, low–calorie or low–sodium version?
2. Are all the ingredients – especially those high in fat – essential?
3. Can the recipe be cooked by a method that's lower in fat?
4. Will the recipe work if high–fat ingredients are reduced or eliminated?

Remember, most recipes will contain some fat — the goal is to decrease the total amount of fat without sacrificing taste and texture.

For a quick lesson in modifying recipes for healthier results, compare the original and light version of *Garlic Shrimp on a Bun*. Then, take what you've learned and apply it to some of your favorite recipes. Don't be afraid to experiment — you'll be surprised just how often experiments turn into favorite recipes. Of course, we all have an occasional flop — just keep trying!

Garlic Shrimp on a Bun

¼ c. green onion, chopped   OK

2–3 cloves garlic, minced   OK

~~1 c. butter, melted~~   *2 tsp. olive oil*

1 T. white wine   *increase to 2/3 cup*

1 tsp. lemon juice   *increase to 1/4 cup*

⅛ tsp. salt   OK

⅛ tsp. pepper   OK

1 tsp. dried dillweed   OK

1 ½ lbs. large fresh shrimp, unpeeled   OK

2 French rolls, split lengthwise, ~~brushed with butter~~ and toasted

Saute' onions and garlic in butter until onions are tender. Add wine, lemon juice, salt, pepper and dillweed; bring to a boil and let simmer 5 minutes to blend flavors. Add shrimp and cook 5 minutes longer until shrimp are done. Spoon over toasted rolls and serve immediately.

When your recipe calls for:	Try this:

MEAT & MEAT ALTERNATIVES:

1 whole egg	2 egg whites or $1/4$ cup egg substitute
2 strips of bacon	1 oz. lean ham or Canadian bacon
Ground beef	Extra–lean ground beef or ground turkey
Expensive high–fat meats	Inexpensive Select grade meats, trimmed of excess fat
Chicken with skin	Remove skin before cooking
Oil packed tuna	Water packed tuna

DAIRY PRODUCTS:

Whole milk	1% or skim milk
Cream	Evaporated skim milk
Sour cream	Plain low–fat yogurt or blended cottage cheese
Cream cheese	Low–fat or dry curd cottage cheese
Cheddar cheese	Extra–sharp Cheddar cheese, half amount
American, Cheddar, Colby, Monterey Jack and Swiss cheeses	A cheese with 5 or fewer grams of fat per ounce
Mozzarella cheese	Part–skim mozzarella cheese
Ricotta cheese	Lite ricotta or part–skim ricotta cheese
Ice cream	Frozen yogurt or ice milk
Whipped cream	Evaporated skim milk, chilled until almost frozen, then whipped

FRUIT:

Jam, jelly or preserves	Fruit spreads or sugar–reduced preserves
Syrup packed fruit	Fruit packed in own juice or water packed

FATS:

$1/2$ cup shortening	$1/3$ cup oil
Mayonnaise	Fat–free mayonnaise, light mayonnaise or plain nonfat yogurt
1 cup butter	Margarine or $2/3$ cup oil
Baking chocolate	3 tablespoons cocoa plus 1 tablespoon vegetable margarine
Fudge sauce	Chocolate syrup
Nuts	Reduce amount by $1/3$–$1/2$
Salad dressing	Oil–free salad dressing
Canned condensed cream soups	99% fat–free condensed cream soups
Grease a pan	Coat pan with cooking spray

Table of Contents

APPETIZERS & SNACKS

APPETIZERS & SNACKS

Nutty Apricot Cheese Spread

This unusual combination of flavors melds together for an outstanding spread that's sure to get rave reviews!

1 tub (8 oz.) fat–free cream cheese
$\frac{1}{2}$ c. reduced–sugar apricot preserves
or spread
$\frac{1}{4}$ c. green onion, sliced
$\frac{1}{4}$ c. dry roasted peanuts, coarsely chopped

Run a knife around the outer edge of cream cheese to loosen; place it on a serving plate. Spread apricot preserves over cream cheese; top with green onion and peanuts. Serve immediately or refrigerate up to 1 hour. Serve with Melba rounds or other low–fat crackers.

Yield:
  8 servings
Serving Size:
  2 tablespoons
Preparation Time:
  5 minutes

Nutrient Analysis per serving:

Calories: 76.5
Fat: 2.3 gm
Cholesterol: 5 mg
Sodium: 306 mg

Fat–free cream cheese works great in recipes that aren't cooked. Cooking with it is tricky because its texture produces a much softer product. Use fat–free cream cheese only in recipes that have been tested with it.

Colorado Crab Spread

Double the recipe and serve this delicious appetizer as a light supper.

Yield:
   3 cups
   6 servings

Serving Size:
   ¹/₂ cup

Preparation Time:
   15 minutes

Nutrient Analysis per serving:

Calories: 122
Fat: 6 gm
Cholesterol: 2 mg
Sodium: 194 mg

1 lb. imitation crabmeat
2 T. lemon juice
2 T. plain nonfat yogurt
¹/₄ c. fat–free mayonnaise
¹/₂ tsp. dried dillweed
¹/₄ tsp. celery salt
¹/₂ c. bell pepper, finely chopped
¹/₄ c. red onion, finely chopped
¹/₂ tsp. garlic powder

In medium–sized bowl, cut crab into small pieces; toss with lemon juice. Add remaining ingredients and mix well. Serve with low–fat crackers.

Imitation crabmeat, or surimi, is made from mild flavored fish such as pollack or cod, to which crab flavoring is added — giving the product a distinctive crab taste without the high price.

Cool Garden Pizza

*This make–ahead pizza is fun to take along
for a picnic or concert at Red Rocks Park.*

1 loaf frozen whole wheat bread dough, thawed
1 pkg. (8 oz.) fat–free cream cheese, softened
1 pkg. Ranch salad dressing mix
1 ½ c. raw vegetables, finely grated
    (cauliflower, broccoli, zucchini, celery)
½ c. green onion, sliced
½ c. carrot, shredded
½ c. tomato, finely chopped, drained

Preheat oven to 350°. Stretch bread dough into a
15 ½ x 12–inch jellyroll pan and bake until
done (about 15–20 minutes); cool completely.
Blend cream cheese and Ranch dressing mix;
spread evenly on crust. Sprinkle vegetables,
green onion, carrots and tomato over cream
cheese mixture. Press in gently; chill. Cut into 24
bite–sized pieces and serve.

Yield:
    12 servings
Serving Size:
    2 pieces
Preparation Time:
    30–35 minutes
Cooking Time:
    15–20 minutes

**Nutrient Analysis
per serving:**

Calories: 155
Fat: 6 gm
Cholesterol: 8 mg
Sodium: 313 mg

*You would have to
eat about 32 cups of
air–popped popcorn
(unbuttered) to equal
the 840 calories in a
cup of peanuts.*

Fresh Tomato Antipasto

This authentic Italian recipe is impressive
— and so easy.

Yield:
   2 cups
   8 servings

Serving Size:
   1/4 cup

Preparation Time:
   7–10 minutes

1 lb. ripe tomatoes, chopped (about 3 medium)
2 cloves garlic, minced
2 T. fresh basil leaves, finely chopped
1/8 c. fresh parsley, chopped
1 T. olive oil
Salt and freshly ground black pepper, to taste

Lightly salt tomatoes and let them drain in colander. Combine garlic, basil and parsley; mix with olive oil. Season to taste with salt and pepper. Toss tomatoes and herb mixture; set aside. Serve with Melba toast rounds.

**Nutrient Analysis
per serving:**

Calories: 29
Fat: 1.8 gm
Cholesterol: 0 mg
Sodium: 79 mg

Dried herbs taste stronger than fresh because the flavor is more concentrated. A good rule of thumb for substitution is to use 1 teaspoon dried herbs for 1 tablespoon fresh.

6

Chili Popcorn

Easy and good! Keep on hand in an airtight container for snacks.

6 c. air–popped corn
1 T. margarine, melted
1/2 tsp. chili powder
1/8 tsp salt
1/8 tsp. garlic powder

While popcorn is popping, combine margarine, chili powder, salt and garlic powder. Drizzle mixture over warm popcorn. Toss gently to coat.

Yield:
6 cups
6 servings

Serving Size:
1 cup

Preparation Time:
2–5 minutes

Nutrient Analysis per serving:

Calories: 64
Fat: 2.5 gm
Cholesterol: 0 mg
Sodium: 74 mg

Crunchy Snack Mix

6 c. air–popped corn
1 c. *Crispix* or *Rice Chex* cereal
1 c. tiny pretzels
1 c. *Cheerios* cereal
1 c. *Multi–Bran Chex* cereal
2 T. margarine, melted
1 tsp. Worcestershire sauce
1/2 tsp. garlic salt
1/2 tsp. onion powder

Preheat oven to 300°. Combine first 5 ingredients in a large bowl. Combine margarine and Worcestershire sauce; drizzle over popcorn mixture. Toss well. Sprinkle garlic salt and onion powder over popcorn mixture; toss well. Spread mixture in a 15½ x 12-inch jellyroll pan and bake for 10 minutes, stirring once. Turn off oven and let mixture cool in oven. Store in airtight container.

Yield:
10 cups
10 servings

Serving Size:
1 cup

Preparation Time:
20 minutes

Cooking Time:
10 minutes

Cooling Time:
1 hour

Nutrient Analysis per serving:

Calories: 105
Fat: 3.2 gm
Cholesterol: 0 mg
Sodium: 336 mg

Spicy Corn Dip

A colorful appetizer for just about any occasion.

Yield:
    2 cups
    8 servings

Serving Size:
    ¼ cup

Preparation Time:
    15 minutes

1 can (12 oz.) mexicorn, drained
1 medium fresh tomato, chopped
¼ c. onion, chopped
2 jalapeno peppers, seeded and chopped
2 T. fat–free mayonnaise

Stir all ingredients together in a small bowl. Serve with Melba toast rounds.

Nutrient Analysis per serving:

Calories: 46
Fat: .3 gm
Cholesterol: 0 mg
Sodium: 154 mg

You may be surprised to learn that canned and frozen produce may, in some cases, be more nutritious than fresh. By the time vegetables are picked, packaged, shipped to a warehouse, transported to the supermarket, purchased and then placed in the refrigerator or on the counter for several days before being served, they are no longer fresh.

Cajun–Style Garbanzo Nuts

This spicy snack also makes a good salad topper.

1 can (15 ½ oz.) garbanzo beans
Cooking spray
½–1 tsp. pepper
1 tsp. garlic powder
¼–½ tsp. cayenne pepper
¼ tsp. dried whole oregano
1/2 tsp. salt (optional)

Preheat oven to 325°. Drain and rinse beans. Spread beans on a baking sheet that has been coated with cooking spray. In a small bowl combine all spices. While beans are moist, sprinkle with spice mixture. Bake for 45–55 minutes, or until browned and crisp. Stir as needed to brown evenly.

Yield:
1⅓ cups
4 servings

Serving Size:
⅓ cup

Preparation Time:
5 minutes

Cooking Time:
45–55 minutes

Nutrient Analysis per serving:

Calories: 134
Fat: 1.3 gm
Cholesterol: 0 mg
Sodium: 328 mg

Garbanzo Nuts make a great snack or salad topping. While regular nuts are about 77% fat, our Garbanzo Nuts are only 9% fat.

Curry Dip

*Curry adds the exotic flavor of India
to your menu with this favorite.*

Yield:
  1 1/4 cups
  10 servings

Serving Size:
  2 tablespoons

Preparation Time:
  5 minutes

**Nutrient Analysis
per serving:**

Calories: 19
Fat: .9 gm
Cholesterol: 1 mg
Sodium: 95 mg

1 c. plain nonfat yogurt
3 T. light mayonnaise
2 tsp. curry powder
1/4 tsp. onion salt

Mix all ingredients together and chill. Serve as a dip with assorted vegetables or as a sauce with fish or chicken.

Dilly Dip

*The delicate flavor of this dip is ideal
when served with crudites for a picnic
in the mountains.*

Yield:
  1-1/4 cups
  10 servings

Serving Size:
  2 tablespoons

Preparation Time:
  5 minutes

**Nutrient Analysis
per serving:**

Calories: 19
Fat: .9 gm
Cholesterol: 1 mg
Sodium: 100 mg

1 c. plain nonfat yogurt
3 T. light mayonnaise
2 T. green onion, sliced
1/2 tsp. dried dillweed
1/4 tsp. onion salt
2 tsp. lemon juice
1/2 tsp. Dijon mustard
Pinch of sugar

Mix all ingredients together and chill for 20 minutes to let flavors blend. Serve as a dip with assorted vegetables.

*Substituting plain
nonfat yogurt for
sour cream creates
a savings of 300
calories and 40 grams
of fat in just one cup.*

10

Spinach Dip in Rye

*A simple and delicious dip
with an elegant presentation.*

1 pkg. (10 oz.) frozen chopped spinach,
   thawed and well drained
1 c. plain nonfat yogurt
$1/3$ c. fat–free mayonnaise
1 pkg. dry onion soup mix
Hot pepper sauce, to taste
1 tsp. lemon juice
$1/4$ tsp. pepper
1 round rye loaf

Yield:
   3 cups
   24 servings

Serving Size:
   2 tablespoons

Preparation Time:
   10 minutes

Drain spinach and pat out excess moisture
between two paper towels. Combine spinach
with yogurt, mayonnaise, onion soup mix, hot
pepper sauce, lemon juice and pepper. Chill.
Prepare bread by cutting a bowl from the center
of the loaf. Cut removed bread into 1-inch
cubes. Fill bread bowl with dip and serve with
rye bread cubes and vegetables.

*Nutrient Analysis
per serving:*

Calories: 15
Fat: .7 gm
Cholesterol: 1 mg
Sodium: 133 mg

*Using fat–free
mayonnaise is a great
way to reduce fat and
calories in your favo-
rite recipes. Every
tablespoon of fat–free
mayonnaise substituted
for regular mayonnaise
will save 88 calories
and 12 grams of fat.*

Sweet & Sour Meatballs

*Your guests will love the surprise
in each meatball.*

Yield:
  64 meatballs
  32 servings

Serving Size:
  2 meatballs

Preparation Time:
  30–35 minutes

Cooking Time:
  30 minutes

**Nutrient Analysis
per serving:**

Calories: 56
Fat: .9 gm
Cholesterol: 20 mg
Sodium: 38 mg

2 lbs. lean ground turkey
1 egg
¾ c. onion, finely chopped
Salt and pepper to taste
1 can (8 oz.) whole water chestnuts, quartered

SAUCE:
1 jar (12 oz.) chili sauce
6 oz. grape jelly

Mix meat, egg, onion and seasonings together. Roll mixture into small balls around one–quarter of a water chestnut. Brown in a nonstick skillet. In a large saucepan, mix chili sauce and grape jelly; heat. Add meatballs and simmer for 30 minutes. Serve warm in a chafing dish.

*Nutrition questions?
Call your nearest
registered dietitian
or the Colorado
Dietetic Association.*

Cripple Creek Caviar

Eating black–eyed peas will bring you good luck, that's why this recipe is named after a favorite Colorado gambling town.

1 can (16 oz.) black–eyed peas, drained
   and rinsed
1/3 c. oil–free Italian dressing
1 can (4 oz.) chopped green chilies
1 T. vinegar
1/4 tsp. Italian seasoning
Dash crushed red pepper flakes
2 tomatoes, chopped
1/4 c. green onion, sliced

Combine first 6 ingredients; cover and chill 4–6 hours. Add tomato and green onion; toss gently. Serve with *Pita Wedges* (page 19) or Melba rounds.

Yield:
  2 1/2 cups
  10 servings
Serving Size:
  1/4 cup
Preparation Time:
  10 minutes
Chilling Time:
  4–6 hours

Nutrient Analysis per serving:

Calories: 61
Fat: .4 gm
Cholesterol: 0 mg
Sodium: 137 mg

In addition to soluble fiber – the kind that helps lower blood cholesterol – legumes are a rich source of vegetable protein.

Herbed Deviled Eggs

You'll be delighted with this lower–cholesterol version of deviled eggs.

Yield:
  12 servings
Serving Size:
  1 stuffed egg half
Preparation Time:
  10–15 minutes

Nutrient Analysis per serving:

Calories: 44
Fat: 2.8 gm
Cholesterol: 134 mg
Sodium: 56 mg

6 hard cooked eggs
3 T. 1% cottage cheese, drained
2 T. plain nonfat yogurt
1 T. onion, finely chopped
1 tsp. Dijon mustard
¼ tsp. dried dillweed
⅛ tsp. garlic powder
Dash hot pepper sauce
Salt and pepper to taste (optional)

Cut eggs in half. Put half of the yolks in a small bowl; reserve remaining yolks for another use or discard. With fork, mash yolks together with cottage cheese and yogurt. Stir in remaining ingredients. Fill egg halves and chill. If desired, garnish with dill before serving.

*Recommendations to "lower fat and cholesterol" don't mean "never eat meat" or "avoid eggs" because they contain cholesterol. It is the **total** amount of fat and cholesterol in your diet that matters. Balance high–fat food with other foods that contain less fat and cholesterol.*

14

Peach Pizzazz Punch

A delicate peach sensation!

1 can (12 oz.) orange/peach juice concentrate
2 c. lemon juice
4 liters ginger ale
1 pkg.(16 oz.) frozen peach slices

In a large punch bowl, combine juices. Just before serving add ginger ale and frozen peach slices.

Yield:
  5 quarts
  20 servings

Serving Size:
  1 cup

Preparation Time:
  5 minutes

**Nutrient Analysis
per serving:**

Calories: 136
Fat: 0 gm
Cholesterol: 0 mg
Sodium: 23 mg

Lemon–Strawberry Punch

8 oz. frozen lemonade concentrate, thawed
1 pkg. (10 oz.) frozen strawberries, thawed
1 qt. ginger ale or *7–Up*
Ice

Mix lemonade and strawberries together. Add ginger ale and ice just before serving.

Yield:
  10 cups
  20 servings

Serving Size:
  ½ cup

Preparation Time:
  5–10 minutes

**Nutrient Analysis
per serving:**

Calories: 67
Fat: 0 gm
Cholesterol: 0 mg
Sodium: 5 mg

Caraway Jack Potato Skins

*This sporty appetizer tastes even better
than traditional deep–fried "skins."*

Yield:
  24 pieces
  6 servings

Serving Size:
  4 pieces

Preparation Time:
  20–25 minutes

Cooking Time:
  10–15 minutes

3 medium potatoes, baked
Cooking spray
**1/2 c. (2 oz.) reduced–fat Monterey Jack
  cheese, shredded**
**1/2 tsp. <u>each</u> caraway seeds, chili powder
  and paprika**
1 tsp. Parmesan cheese, grated

Preheat oven to 450°. Cut each potato in quarters lengthwise, and then in half crosswise to form 8 sections. Scoop pulp from skins, leaving 1/8-inch in the shells. Reserve pulp for another use or discard. Spray both sides of the skins with cooking spray. Place on baking sheet; bake 10–12 minutes until crisp. (Skins can be made ahead to this point and reheated before filling.) Fill skins with Monterey Jack cheese, then sprinkle with caraway seeds, chili powder, paprika and Parmesan cheese. Place under broiler; heat just until cheese is melted. Serve hot.

**Nutrient Analysis
per serving:**

Calories: 45
Fat: 1.8 gm
Cholesterol: 4 mg
Sodium: 40 mg

*Potatoes are
naturally rich in
complex carbo-
hydrates, potassium
and vitamin C. Eating
potato skins gives you
an added bonus of a
healthy dose of fiber.*

16

Yogurt Cheese Spread

*A great substitute for cream cheese
and sour cream!*

1 carton (8 oz.) plain nonfat yogurt

To make yogurt cheese, place plain nonfat yogurt in a colander lined with cheesecloth or a coffee filter. Place colander over bowl and cover loosely with plastic wrap; chill 12–24 hours. Discard liquid drained from yogurt; yogurt cheese will remain in colander. For best results, choose nonfat or low-fat yogurt without gelatin.

Variations:

Strawberry Yogurt Cheese Spread

Top your bagel with this delicious spread.

1/2 c. yogurt cheese
2 T. reduced–sugar strawberry preserves
    or spread

Blend together yogurt cheese and strawberry preserves. Spread on breads instead of butter or cream cheese.

Herb Yogurt Cheese Spread

*Spread this on your sandwich instead of
high–fat mayo!*

1/2 c. yogurt cheese
1/2 tsp. dried dillweed or Italian seasoning

Blend together yogurt cheese and seasoning. Chill for 1–2 hours to let flavors blend.

Yield:
 1/2 cup
Serving Size:
 1 tablespoon
Preparation Time:
 3 minutes
Draining Time:
 12–24 hours

*Nutrient Analysis
per serving:*

Calories: 11
Fat: 0 gm
Cholesterol: 0 mg
Sodium: 15 mg

Stuff It!

An elegant appetizer of stuffed cherry tomatoes will add color and excitement to your party fair.

Salmon-Stuffed Tomatoes

Yield:
  18 tomatoes
Serving Size:
  1 tomato
Preparation Time:
  15 minutes

18 cherry tomatoes
6 oz. smoked salmon
$^1/_3$ c. fat-free cream cheese
$^1/_2$ tsp. Worcestershire sauce

Cut tops off of each tomato. Scoop out pulp, leaving shells intact. Invert tomato shells on paper towels to drain. Combine salmon, cream cheese and worcestershire sauce; stir well. Spoon 1 $^1/_2$ teaspoons of stuffing into each tomato. Chill and serve.

Nutrient Analysis per serving:

Calories: 23
Fat: .4 gm
Cholesterol: 2 mg
Sodium: 96 mg

Seasoned Cheese–Stuffed Tomatoes

Nutrient Analysis per serving:

Calories: 13
Fat: .1 gm
Cholesterol: 0 mg
Sodium: 46 mg

18 cherry tomatoes
8 oz. 1 % cottage cheese, drained
1 T. green onions, finely chopped
$^1/_2$ tsp. caraway seed
$^1/_4$ tsp. seasoned salt

Cut tops off of each tomato. Scoop out pulp, leaving shells intact. Invert tomato shells on paper towels to drain. Combine cottage cheese, onion, caraway seeds and salt; stir well. Spooon 1 $^1/_2$ teaspoons of stuffing into each tomato. Chill and serve.

Pita Wedges with Italian Sauce

3 whole wheat pita bread loaves
Olive oil cooking spray
1 tsp. cumin
1 tsp. lemon–pepper seasoning
1 c. commercial low–fat spaghetti sauce

Cut each pita loaf into 8 wedges. Separate each wedge into 2 pieces and place on cookie sheet. Spray the inside of each piece with the olive oil cooking spray. Sprinkle wedges with seasonings and broil until crisp (about 3 minutes) being careful not to overcook. Heat spaghetti sauce and serve as dip for pita wedges.

Yield:
  24 servings
Serving Size:
  1 wedge with
  2 teaspoons sauce
Preparation Time:
  5 minutes
Cooking Time:
  3 minutes

Nutrient Analysis per serving:

Calories: 26
Fat: .2 gm
Cholesterol: 0 mg
Sodium: 34 mg

*No **one** food supplies all the essential nutrients in the amounts you need. So it is important that you eat a variety of foods each day to get the nutrients you need. Make sure your day includes lowfat dairy products, lean meat, plenty of fruits and vegetables, and whole grain breads and cereals.*

Stuffed Mushrooms Florentine

An elegant appetizer for a special occasion.

Yield:
  20 mushrooms
  10 servings

Serving Size:
  2 mushrooms

Preparation Time:
  10 minutes

Cooking Time:
  20 minutes

1 pkg. (10 oz.) frozen chopped spinach, thawed
1 c. herb seasoned bread stuffing cubes
1 egg
1 T. margarine, melted
¼ c. Parmesan cheese, grated
½ T. pepper
1 tsp. garlic salt
¼ tsp. thyme
20 fresh mushrooms

Preheat oven to 350°. Drain spinach and pat out excess moisture between two paper towels. Combine all ingredients, except mushrooms; mix well. Clean mushrooms; remove stems and discard. Evenly spoon stuffing into each mushroom cap. Bake on an ungreased cookie sheet for 15–20 minutes.

Nutrient Analysis per serving:

Calories: 86
Fat: 3 gm
Cholesterol: 28 mg
Sodium: 194 mg

Store loose mushrooms in the refrigerator in a paper bag or open container loosely covered! Mushrooms stored in plastic bags deteriorate quickly.

Oven–Fried Zucchini Sticks

Dunked in spaghetti sauce or plain — even kids will love these.

¼ c. Italian breadcrumbs
1 T. Parmesan cheese, grated
⅛ tsp. garlic powder
2 medium zucchini
1 tsp. olive oil
3 T. water
Cooking spray
1 c. commercial low–fat spaghetti sauce

Preheat oven to 475°. Combine breadcrumbs, Parmesan cheese and garlic powder in a shallow dish; set aside. Cut each zucchini lengthwise into 4 pieces; cut each piece in half crosswise. Place pieces in zip–top bag. Add oil and water; shake. Dredge zucchini in breadcrumb mixture and place on baking sheet coated with cooking spray. Bake for 10 minutes or until brown and tender. Serve with warm spaghetti sauce.

Yield:
  16 sticks
  8 servings

Serving Size:
  2 sticks

Preparation Time:
  15 minutes

Cooking Time:
  10 minutes

***Nutrient Analysis
per serving:***

Calories: 38
Fat: 1.3 gm
Cholesterol: 1 mg
Sodium: 34 mg

Leading health authorities agree that eating at least five fruits and vegetables daily is important for good health. Eat a variety of fruits and vege-tables to get the vitamin C, vitamin A and fiber your body needs.

Savory Stuffed Mushrooms

*Everyone will be reaching
for this flavorful appetizer.*

Yield:
  16 mushrooms
  8 servings

Serving Size:
  2 mushrooms

Preparation Time:
  25 minutes

Cooking Time:
  15–20 minutes

**Nutrient Analysis
per serving:**

Calories: 83
Fat: 2 gm
Cholesterol: 7 mg
Sodium: 182 mg

16 large mushrooms
Cooking spray
$^1/_4$ c. green pepper, finely chopped
$^1/_4$ c. onion, finely chopped
1 $^1/_2$ c. soft breadcrumbs, (about 4 slices)
**$^1/_2$ c. (2 oz.) reduced–fat Monterey Jack
  cheese, shredded**
$^1/_2$ tsp. salt
$^1/_2$ tsp. dried whole thyme
$^1/_4$ tsp. turmeric
$^1/_4$ tsp. pepper

Preheat oven to 350°. Clean mushrooms and remove stems. Finely chop $^1/_3$ cup stems, reserving remaining stems for another use. Set mushroom caps aside. Saute chopped stems, green pepper and onion in a nonstick skillet coated with cooking spray until tender. Remove from heat; stir in remaining ingredients (except mushroom caps). Evenly spoon stuffing into each reserved mushroom cap. Bake for 15–20 minutes.

Hint: Mushrooms may be stuffed ahead of time and kept in refrigerator until ready to bake.

*Never wash mush-
rooms until you are
ready to use them.
To wash, simply
wipe them with a
damp paper towel.*

Teriyaki Ribbons

For a unique appetizer with a distinctive oriental flavor, add this to your menu.

1 ½ lbs. flank steak
¾ c. Teriyaki sauce
2 large cloves garlic, minced
1 tsp. ginger
1 tsp. crushed red pepper flakes

Cut steak diagonally, against the grain, into ¼-inch slices. (Slicing is easiest when beef has been put in the freezer for 1 hour and is partially frozen.) Combine Teriyaki and seasonings. Marinate steak for 1 hour in Teriyaki marinade. Lace steak slices on bamboo skewers. Broil or grill skewers on both sides until done.

Yield:
48 ribbons
24 servings

Serving Size:
2 skewers

Preparation Time:
5–10 minutes

Marinating Time:
1 hour

Cooking Time:
8–10 minutes

Nutrient Analysis per serving:

Calories: 50
Fat: 2.5 gm
Cholesterol: 12 mg
Sodium: 181 mg

To keep bamboo skewers from burning while the meat is cooking, soak them in water for 15 minutes before threading the meat.

Mexican Artichoke Dip

An old favorite with a Southwestern twist.

Yield:
  3½ cups
  14 servings

Serving Size:
  1/4 cup

Preparation Time:
  15 minutes

Cooking Time:
  12–20 minutes

1 c. fat–free mayonnaise
½ c. Parmesan cheese, grated
1 c. soft breadcrumbs
¼ tsp. Worcestershire sauce
¼ tsp. hot pepper sauce
⅛ tsp. garlic powder
2 cans (14 oz. each) artichoke hearts, drained and finely chopped
1 can (4 oz.) chopped green chilies
Cooking spray

Nutrient Analysis per serving:

Calories: 101
Fat: 1.4 gm
Cholesterol: 2 mg
Sodium: 551 mg

Preheat oven to 350°. Combine mayonnaise, Parmesan cheese, breadcrumbs, Worcestershire sauce, hot pepper sauce and garlic powder; gently fold in artichokes and green chilies. Spoon mixture into a 1-quart casserole dish coated with cooking spray. Cover and bake for 20 minutes. Serve with *Pita Wedges* (page 19), Melba rounds or vegetable sticks.

Microwave instructions: Microwave on MEDIUM (50% power) for 12–14 minutes, stirring halfway through cooking time.

Fat–free mayonnaise can be substituted for regular mayonnaise in highly flavored salads, dips and on sandwiches. However, cooking with it may not produce the same quality product as you might expect. To be safe, follow recipes such as this one that have been tested using fat–free mayonnaise.

24

BRUNCH

BRUNCH

Swedish Pancakes with Cointreau Strawberries

This light pancake will soon be a favorite for a weekend treat.

2 c. strawberries, sliced
2 T. Cointreau or orange–flavored liqueur
2 eggs, beaten
2 egg whites
1 $\frac{1}{3}$ c. skim milk
2 T. oil
1 c. flour
$\frac{1}{2}$ tsp. salt
Cooking spray

Mix strawberries and Cointreau; set aside. Combine eggs, milk and oil; add flour and salt. Stir with wire whisk to eliminate lumps. Coat a small nonstick skillet with cooking spray. Place skillet over medium heat. Pour only enough batter into skillet to coat pan bottom. When batter is set and browned; flip pancake. Remove from skillet after both sides are light brown. Serve hot with *Cointreau Strawberry* topping.

Yield:
12 pancakes
4 servings

Serving Size:
3 pancakes

Preparation Time:
10 minutes

Cooking Time:
15–20 minutes

Nutrient Analysis per serving:

Calories: 280
Fat: 9.5 gm
Cholesterol: 93 mg
Sodium: 192 mg

Two average–size kiwis have more potassium than a 6-inch banana, more dietary fiber than a $\frac{2}{3}$-cup serving of bran flakes, nearly twice as much vitamin C as an orange, and twice the vitamin E of an avocado — and only 90 calories.

Spicy Oat Pancakes

Yield:
10 pancakes
5 servings

Serving Size:
2 pancakes

Preparation Time:
5–10 minutes

Cooking Time:
4–5 minutes

Nutrient Analysis per serving:

Calories: 204
Fat: 7.8 gm
Cholesterol: 55 mg
Sodium: 282 mg

¾ c. regular oats, uncooked
¾ c. whole wheat flour
1 ½ tsp. baking powder
¾ tsp. cinnamon
¼ tsp. ginger
¼ tsp. baking soda
1 egg
1 c. skim milk
2 T. oil
1 T. honey or molasses

In a bowl, combine oats, flour, baking powder, cinnamon, ginger and baking soda. In another bowl, mix egg, milk, oil and honey; mix until blended and smooth. Combine dry and liquid ingredients and stir just until blended. Coat hot griddle with cooking spray. Pour a scant ¼ cup of batter onto griddle. Cook until bubbles start to burst on first side; flip pancake and cook other side.

While putting all of your eggs in one basket was never a good idea, neither is taking them out of the egg carton. Eggs left uncovered in the refrigerator can absorb odors from the foods around them, and that can ruin their flavor.

Wild Mountain Blueberry Pancakes

1 c. low–fat buttermilk or plain nonfat yogurt
1 egg
$^1/_2$ tsp. vanilla
1 c. whole wheat flour
1 T. sugar
1 tsp. baking powder
$^1/_2$ tsp. baking soda
1 c. blueberries, washed and drained
Cooking spray

In a large bowl, combine buttermilk, egg and vanilla. In a separate bowl, combine remaining dry ingredients. Mix dry ingredients into bowl with liquid ingredients. Fold in blueberries. Pour $^1/_4$ cup of batter onto a hot nonstick skillet coated with cooking spray. When bubbles begin to burst on first side, flip and cook other side of pancake until golden brown. Serve warm.

Yield:
   12 pancakes
   4 servings

Serving Size:
   3 pancakes

Preparation Time:
   10 minutes

Cooking Time:
   15–20 minutes

Nutrient Analysis per serving:

Calories: 172
Fat: 2.2 gm
Cholesterol: 47 mg
Sodium: 368 mg

Overmixed pancake batter can over-develop the gluten in the flour and cause pancakes to be tough.

Oatmeal Apple Griddle Cakes

A great use for leftover oatmeal.

Yield:
    12 pancakes
    4 servings

Serving Size:
    3 pancakes

Preparation Time:
    15 minutes

Cooking Time:
    15–20 minutes

Nutrient Analysis per serving:

Calories: 247
Fat: 9.5 gm
Cholesterol: 69 mg
Sodium: 504 mg

½ c. flour
2 T. sugar
1 tsp. baking powder
½ tsp. salt
1 ½ c. cooked oatmeal
1 egg
¾ c. skim milk
2 T. oil
1 c. apple, finely chopped
Cooking spray

Sift together flour, sugar, baking powder and salt; add remaining ingredients and stir until moistened. Pour batter onto a hot griddle coated with cooking spray. When bubbles start to burst on first side, flip pancake and cook other side.

Breakfast is the most important meal of the day. It doesn't have to be elaborate, but it should be high in nutrition to get your day off to a healthy start.

Cranberry–Orange Pancakes

*Serve this favorite to a crowd
celebrating the holidays.*

1 c. fresh cranberries, washed

1/2 c. orange juice

1 c. flour

1 c. whole wheat flour

2 tsp. baking powder

1/2 tsp. baking soda

1 T. sugar

1/4 tsp. salt

2 T. oil

3 eggs

1 c. skim milk

1/2 c. walnuts, chopped (optional)

Cooking spray

Combine cranberries and orange juice in small saucepan. Bring to a boil and simmer until cranberries are soft (about 5 minutes). Let cool. Combine all dry ingredients; set aside. In a large mixing bowl, beat together oil, eggs and milk. Stir in dry ingredients then stir in cranberry/ orange juice mixture. Pour 1/4 cup of batter onto a hot griddle coated with cooking spray. Cook until bubbles start to burst on first side, then flip pancake and continue to cook until golden brown.

Yield:
24 pancakes
8 servings

Serving Size:
3 pancakes

Preparation Time:
20 minutes

Cooking Time:
15 minutes

**Nutrient Analysis
per serving:**

Calories: 184
Fat: 5.3 gm
Cholesterol: 69 mg
Sodium: 326 mg

If you like cranberries year 'round — buy extra when they're in season, double–wrap the bag with plastic wrap and freeze them up to nine months.

Oat Bran Waffles

These high–fiber waffles are delicious anytime of the day or night, especially when served with Cran–Raspberry Topping.

Yield:
4 servings

Serving Size:
1 waffle

Preparation Time:
5 minutes

Cooking Time:
10 minutes

Nutrient Analysis per serving:

Calories: 200
Fat: 5 gm
Cholesterol: 1 mg
Sodium: 484 mg

Cooking spray
1 c. Whole Wheat and Honey pancake mix (*Krusteaz* brand)
½ c. uncooked oat bran or regular oats, uncooked
1 c. skim milk
1 T. oil
1 egg white
1 tsp. cinnamon

Coat waffle iron with cooking spray; allow waffle iron to preheat. Mix together pancake mix and oat bran; combine with remaining ingredients. Pour batter onto hot waffle iron. Bake until steaming stops. Lift waffle from iron with fork.

Variation: For a lighter waffle, beat egg white and fold into mixture.

Traditional pancake and waffle recipes often use Bisquick. By switching to Krusteaz brand Whole Wheat and Honey, you save 7 grams of fat and increase the fiber 5–fold.

Oven–Baked French Toast

*With this breakfast, you can read the
Sunday paper while it's cooking.*

Cooking spray
8 slices (³/₄-inch thick) French bread
2 eggs, beaten
2 egg whites
¹/₂ c. skim milk
1 ¹/₂ T. orange juice
1 T. brown sugar
¹/₂ tsp. cinnamon
¹/₂ tsp. vanilla
1 T. powdered sugar

Yield:
   8 slices
   4 servings

Serving Size:
   2 slices

Preparation Time:
   10 minutes

Cooking Time:
   10–13 minutes

Preheat oven to 425°. Coat a shallow baking pan with cooking spray; heat pan for 15 minutes or until hot. Meanwhile, combine eggs, egg whites, milk, orange juice, sugar, cinnamon and vanilla; beat well. Dip bread slices into egg mixture, turning to coat evenly. Place dipped bread in hot pan. Bake for 5–7 minutes; turn and bake an additional 5–6 minutes until golden brown. Serve immediately with powdered sugar sprinkled over evenly.

*Nutrient Analysis
per serving:*

Calories: 234
Fat: 3.6 gm
Cholesterol: 93 mg
Sodium: 394 mg

*This recipe for French
toast can also be
cooked on top of the
stove in a nonstick
skillet coated with
cooking spray.*

German Pancake
with Saucy Apples

Impressive to look at — easy to prepare.

Yield:
6 servings

Serving Size:
⅙ of pancake
and apples

Preparation Time:
5–10 minutes

Cooking Time:
20–25 minutes

2 T. margarine
¾ c. skim milk
2 eggs
1 egg white
¾ c. flour

SAUCY APPLES:
5 medium apples, peeled, quartered and cored
3 T. water
2 T. to ⅓ c. brown sugar, packed
1/2 tsp. cinnamon
Dash nutmeg

Nutrient Analysis per serving:

Calories:	206
Fat:	6.3 gm
Cholesterol:	92 mg
Sodium:	94 mg

Preheat oven to 425°. Put margarine in a large oven–proof frying pan and set in oven. Mix batter quickly while margarine melts. Put eggs in blender container and process at high speed for 1 minute. With motor running, pour in milk; slowly add flour. Continue processing for 30 seconds. Remove pan from oven, swirl melted margarine around edges of pan and pour batter into hot frying pan. Return to oven and bake for 10 minutes, then reduce temperature to 350° and bake for an additional 10–15 minutes or until puffy and golden brown. Serve with *Saucy Apples* or a sprinkling of powdered sugar and fresh fruit.

Saucy Apples: In 2 ½-quart glass casserole, combine apples and water. Microwave on high power, covered, for 6–8 minutes (or until soft). Add sugar to taste and mix in cinnamon and nutmeg. In batches (if desired), process in blender or food processor until smooth. Serve warm over *German Pancake.*

High Country
Rhubarb Coffee Cake

*A favorite summer coffeecake with rhubarb,
or substitute cranberries for a winter coffeecake.*

¹/₂ c. brown sugar, packed
¹/₃ c. margarine, softened
1 egg
1 c. whole wheat flour
1 c. flour
1 tsp. baking soda
¹/₄ tsp. salt
1 c. plain nonfat yogurt
1 ¹/₂ c. rhubarb, fresh or frozen, chopped

TOPPING:
¹/₃ c. brown sugar, packed
¹/₄ c. regular oats, uncooked
1 T. margarine, softened
1 tsp. cinnamon

Yield:
   12 servings

Serving Size:
   4x2¹/₂-inch piece

Preparation Time:
   15 minutes

Cooking Time:
   40–50 minutes

*Nutrient Analysis
per serving:*

Calories: 202
Fat: 6.8 gm
Cholesterol: 15 mg
Sodium: 208 mg

Preheat oven to 350°. Cream together brown
sugar, margarine and egg. Stir together flour,
baking soda and salt; add to cream mixture alternately with yogurt. Stir in fruit. Pour into a
greased and floured 12x8x2-inch baking pan.
Mix sugar, oats, margarine and cinnamon until
crumbly; sprinkle over batter. Bake for 40–50
minutes.

*Eating with some
regularity helps
establish eating
patterns and keeps
the appetite under
control, whereas
skipping meals can
lead to overeating*

35

French Coffee Cake

An attractive bundt coffee cake that tastes wonderful by itself or drizzled with powder sugar frosting.

Yield:
16 servings

Serving Size:
1 wedge

Preparation Time:
20–25 minutes

Cooking Time:
45 minutes

Nutrient Analysis per serving:

Calories: 215
Fat: 3.8 gm
Cholesterol: 0 mg
Sodium: 176 mg

2/3 c. reduced–calorie margarine
1 ¼ c. sugar
3 egg whites
1 ½ tsp. vanilla
3 c. flour
1 ½ tsp. baking powder
1 tsp. baking soda
2 c. plain nonfat yogurt

FILLING:
¼ c. walnuts, chopped
¼ c. brown sugar, packed
¼ c. sugar
1 ½ tsp. cinnamon

Preheat oven to 350°. Cream margarine and sugar in a medium bowl with an electric mixer. Add egg whites and vanilla; mix thoroughly. Combine flour, baking powder and baking soda. Gradually add flour mixture to creamed mixture alternately with yogurt, beginning and ending with flour mixture. In a separate bowl, combine filling ingredients, mixing with a fork until crumbly. Pour ⅓ of the batter into a 12–cup bundt pan coated with cooking spray. Sprinkle with half of the nut filling. Repeat layers, ending with batter. Bake for 45 minutes. Cool completely in pan on wire rack, then turn out of the pan and serve.

Country Brunch Casserole

The best brunch casserole — just prepare it the night before and have it ready to pop into the oven for a leisurely brunch.

½ c. onion, chopped
2 T. water
Cooking spray
3 c. bread stuffing cubes
⅓ lb. Canadian Bacon, thinly sliced,
    cut into bite–size pieces
1 c. (4 oz.) sharp reduced–fat Cheddar cheese,
    shredded
3 eggs
2 egg whites
½ tsp. dry mustard
½ tsp. onion salt
2 c. skim milk

Microwave onion and water on HIGH for 2 minutes, stirring occasionally. Place stuffing cubes in bottom of a 12x8x2-inch baking dish that has been coated with a cooking spray. Sprinkle with onion, ham and cheese. In a separate bowl, mix eggs, milk and seasonings; pour over stuffing mixture. Cover and refrigerate overnight. Bake, uncovered, at 325° for 1 hour. Let stand 10 minutes before serving.

Yield:
    8 servings
Serving Size:
    4x3-inch piece
Preparation Time:
    15 minutes
Standing Time:
    10 minutes
Cooking Time:
    1 hour

Nutrient Analysis per serving:

Calories: 287
Fat: 9.7 gm
Cholesterol: 127 mg
Sodium: 506 mg

Canadian bacon contains less than half the fat found in cured bacon. Thinly diced, it is an excellent substitute for sausage and bacon in traditional brunch dishes.

Crustless Vegetable Cheese Pie

No crust to add calories!

Yield:
6 servings

Serving Size:
1/6 of 9-inch pie

Preparation Time:
20 minutes

Cooking Time:
45–50 minutes

Nutrient Analysis per serving:

Calories: 225
Fat: 10 gm
Cholesterol: 165 mg
Sodium: 677 mg

Cooking spray
1/4 lb. fresh mushrooms, sliced
1 small zucchini, cut into 1/2-inch pieces
1 small green pepper, finely chopped
1 lb. 1% cottage cheese
1 c. (4 oz.) part–skim mozzarella cheese, shredded
3 eggs, beaten
1 pkg. frozen chopped spinach, thawed
1 T. dried dillweed
1/4 tsp. garlic salt
1/8 tsp. pepper

Preheat oven to 350°. Spray a large nonstick skillet with cooking spray. Add mushrooms, zucchini and green pepper; sauté until soft. Drain any excess liquid and cool to lukewarm. Combine cheeses, eggs, spinach (with all water squeezed out), dill and mushroom mixture together. Season with garlic salt and pepper; mix well. Place mixture in a 9-inch pie pan coated with cooking spray. Bake about 45–50 minutes, or until knife inserted into comes out clean. Remove from oven and let stand for 5 minutes before serving.

Frozen vegetables are blanched (submerged in boiling water) before they are frozen to destroy naturally–present enzymes that may affect flavor and texture while frozen.

Fritatta Primavera

A delightful egg dish to serve with banana muffins and fresh fruit.

Cooking spray

1 $^1/_2$ c. fresh mushrooms, sliced

1 c. onion, chopped

1 c. tomatoes, diced

1 clove garlic, minced

1 can (14 oz.) quartered artichoke hearts, drained

1 pkg. (10 oz.) frozen spinach, thawed

3 whole eggs

3 egg whites

$^1/_2$ tsp. Italian seasoning

1 c. (4 oz.) sharp reduced–fat Cheddar cheese, grated

Salt and pepper to taste

Yield:
4 servings

Serving Size:
4x4-inch piece

Preparation Time:
20 minutes

Cooking Time:
45 minutes

Nutrient Analysis per serving:

Calories: 158
Fat: 5.7 gm
Cholesterol: 136 mg
Sodium: 641 mg

Preheat oven to 350°. Coat a nonstick skillet with cooking spray. Add mushrooms, onion, tomato and garlic; sauté until tender. Beat eggs, egg whites and Italian seasoning lightly. Combine vegetable mixture, artichokes, spinach, eggs and cheese; stir. Pour mixture into an 8x8x2-inch baking dish coated with cooking spray. Bake 45 minutes or until firm.

Eggs can provide important nutrients to the diet; but egg yolks are high in cholesterol. The American Heart Association recommends no more than 4 egg yolks per week.

Sunday Morning Scramble

A great way to use up that extra baked potato in the fridge.

Yield:
 2 servings

Serving Size:
 about 1 cup

Preparation Time:
 5 minutes

Cooking Time:
 5–7 minutes

Nutrient Analysis per serving:

Calories: 181
Fat: 8 gm
Cholesterol: 190 mg
Sodium: 492 mg

1 medium baked potato, cubed
2 T. green pepper, chopped
2 T. onion, chopped
¼ tsp. garlic salt
¼ tsp. hot pepper sauce
Freshly ground pepper
1 tsp. margarine
2 eggs
2 egg whites
2 tsp. water
¼ c. (1 oz.) part–skim mozzarella cheese, shredded
1 tomato, sliced

Combine potato, green pepper, onion, garlic salt, hot pepper sauce and pepper to taste; sauté in margarine in a nonstick pan for 2 minutes. Beat eggs and egg whites with water; fold gently into potato mixture. Cook, stirring frequently, until softly set. Sprinkle with cheese; serve with sliced tomatoes.

A potato can be cooked quickly in a microwave oven by piercing the potato with a fork and cooking on HIGH power for 4–6 minutes. Turn potato after the first 2–3 minutes.

Breakfast Burritos

A quick breakfast when you're running late — keep your freezer stocked with these.

1 T. oil
1 medium onion, chopped
1 bag (2 lb.) frozen O'Brien Potatoes
8 eggs, beaten
4 egg whites
½ c. skim milk
1 can (7 oz.) chopped green chilies
1 c. picante sauce
20 flour tortillas, warmed
Salsa (optional)

Yield:
20 burritos
20 servings

Serving Size:
1 burrito

Preparation Time:
10 minutes

Cooking Time:
15 minutes

In a large nonstick skillet, heat oil. Add onion and cook for 3–4 minutes. To onion add potatoes and continue to cook until potatoes begin to brown, stirring frequently. In a large bowl combine eggs, egg whites and milk; mix well. Pour egg mixture over browned potatoes, stir in green chilies and scramble until eggs are cooked. Assemble burritos by spooning about ⅓ cup of mixture onto warm tortilla, spoon picante sauce over each and roll into a burrito. Serve alone or with salsa.

Hint: Breakfast burritos freeze well and can be defrosted by wrapping in a paper towel and microwaving at 50% power for 3 minutes each.

Nutrient Analysis per serving:

Calories: 185
Fat: 5.1 gm
Cholesterol: 109 mg
Sodium: 231 mg

When buying flour tortillas, check the ingredient list and choose ones that contain vegetable oil, a polyunsaturated fat, rather than those made with lard, a saturated fat. Also, look for whole wheat tortillas, available in most grocery stores.

Backpack Muesli

Hearty, warm breakfast for the backcountry.

Yield:
4 cups
4 servings

Serving Size:
1 cup

Preparation Time:
7 minutes

Cooking Time:
5 minutes

**Nutrient Analysis
per serving:**

Calories: 314
Fat: 7.9 gm
Cholesterol: 2 mg
Sodium: 88 mg

1 c. regular oats, uncooked
1 c. shredded whole wheat cereal, crushed
¹/₄ c. raisins
¹/₄ c. coconut
¹/₄ c. dried apples, chopped
¹/₄ c. nuts or seeds
²/₃ c. nonfat dry milk powder
1 tsp. cinnamon
3 c. water

Mix dry ingredients in a plastic bag for camping. In the evening, add 3 cups of water, cover mixture and soak all night. In the morning, heat to boiling over the fire. Add more nonfat dry milk if desired.

Muesli can be stored in a cool, dry place for up to one month. Or, store in a zip–top bag in the refrigerator up to three months.

Fruit Kabobs
and Honey Yogurt

1 pt. whole strawberries, cleaned

1 cantaloupe, halved, seeded, cut from rind
   into 1" cubes

2 kiwi, quartered and cut from rind

1-1/2 c. pineapple, cut in 1" sections

1 (8 oz.) carton low–fat honey vanilla yogurt

Thread fruits onto skewers; chill. Serve with yogurt as a fruit dip.

Yield:
   8 skewers
   8 servings

Serving Size:
   1 skewer

Preparation Time:
   10 minutes

Nutrient Analysis per serving:

Calories: 82
Fat: .9 gm
Cholesterol: 1 mg
Sodium: 25 mg

Cran–Raspberry Topping

When it's cranberry season,
this topping is a must!

1 lb. fresh cranberries, finely chopped

2 tart green apples, peeled, cored
   and minced

3/4 c. sugar

1/2 c. orange marmalade

1 pkg. (10 oz.) frozen raspberries,
   thawed and drained

1 tsp. lemon juice

In a large bowl, combine all ingredients. Serve over waffles, pancakes, or frozen yogurt. Keeps for up to one week when refrigerated.

Yield:
   6 cups
   18 servings

Serving Size:
   1/3 cup

Preparation Time:
   10 minutes

Nutrient Analysis per serving:

Calories: 84
Fat: .2 gm
Cholesterol: 0 mg
Sodium: 1 mg

Turkey Sausage

The flavor of sausage without the fat!
You'll want to make an extra batch to freeze
and have on hand for egg dishes.

Yield:
4 servings

Serving Size:
1 patty

Preparation Time:
5 minutes

Cooking Time:
10 minutes

Nutrient Analysis per serving:

Calories: 77
Fat: 2.1 gm
Cholesterol: 32 mg
Sodium: 116 mg

$^1/_2$ **lb. ground turkey**
1 egg white
1 tsp. Italian seasoning
$^1/_2$ **tsp. fennel seed (optional)**
$^1/_8$ **tsp. salt**

Combine all ingredients in a small bowl; mix well. Shape mixture into 4 patties and chill at least one hour. Coat a large skillet with cooking spray; place over medium heat until hot. Place patties in skillet; cook 5 minutes on each side or until done. Place cooked patties on paper towels to drain; serve warm.

In traditional breakfast sausage, about 76% of calories come from fat. This adjusted recipe provides only 47% of its calories from fat.

44

SOUPS

SOUPS

Carrot–Cashew Soup

*Serve with Quick Yeast Rolls and a salad
for a cozy meal at home.*

4 c. carrots, grated
1 c. onions, chopped
2 T. oil
6 c. chicken stock
1 can (6 oz.) tomato paste
1 c. apples, chopped
$1/3$ c. brown rice
$1/3$ c. cashews
$1/2$ c. raisins (optional)

In a large pot sauté carrots and onions in oil until vegetables are soft, but not browned. Stir in stock, tomato paste, apples and bring the mixture to a boil. Stir in brown rice, reduce heat to a simmer, cover and cook for 45 minutes or until rice is tender. Right before serving, stir in cashews and raisins (if desired).

Yield:
  6 servings
Serving Size:
  1 cup
Preparation Time:
  10–15 minutes
Cooking Time:
  50 minutes

*Nutrient Analysis
per serving:*

Calories: 225
Fat: 10.2 gm
Cholesterol: 0 mg
Sodium: 123 mg

Studies done on more than 1,000 dietitians found that those who started meals with hot soup ate fewer calories than those who skipped the soup course.

Hearty Lentil Stew

A special recipe from the Date Bar restaurant in Colorado Springs.

Yield:
  10 servings

Serving Size:
  1 ¼ cups

Preparation Time:
  30 minutes

Cooking Time:
  45 minutes

Nutrient Analysis per serving:

Calories: 213
Fat: .7 gm
Cholesterol: 0 mg
Sodium: 514 mg

1 pkg. (16 oz.) lentils
10 c. water
1 onion, chopped
½ c. rice
2 tsp. salt
2 cloves garlic, minced
1 tsp. dried whole oregano
1 tsp. dried parsley flakes
3 large tomatoes, chopped
1 carrot, chopped
1 pkg. (10 oz.) frozen chopped spinach,
   thawed and drained

Wash and sort lentils; drain well. In a large pot, combine lentils, water, onion, rice, salt, garlic, oregano and parsley; bring to boil. Cover and simmer for 25 minutes. Add tomatoes, carrot and spinach. Simmer 20 more minutes or until lentils are tender.

If legumes, such as lentils, are not stored in a cool, dry place, they sometimes develop "hard–shell." When this occurs, it is difficult to re-hydrate the legumes and usually requires excessive cooking.

Easy Tortilla Soup

*Keep these ingredients on hand for
an easy lunch with some zip.*

**1 can (10½ oz.) low–sodium chicken
and rice soup**
**1 can (10 oz.) diced tomatoes and
green chilies** *(Rotel* **brand)**
12 *Oven Tortilla Chips* **(see page 202)
or commercial no–oil tortilla chips**

In a saucepan combine soup and tomatoes with
green chilies. Bring to a boil. Place tortilla chips
in the bottom of two soup bowls, then pour the
soup mixture over them. Serve immediately.

Yield:
2 servings
Serving Size:
1 ¼ cups
Preparation Time:
2 minutes
Cooking Time:
5 minutes

***Nutrient Analysis
per serving:***

Calories: 171
Fat: 3.6 gm
Cholesterol: 0 mg
Sodium: 664 mg

Rocky Mountain Oyster Stew

Not <u>those</u> Rocky Mountain oysters!
<u>Real</u> oyster stew!

Yield:
  4 servings

Serving Size:
  1 ¼ cups

Preparation Time:
  10 minutes

Cooking Time:
  20 minutes

Nutrient Analysis per serving:

Calories: 218
Fat: 9.6 gm
Cholesterol: 61 mg
Sodium: 543 mg

1 ½ doz. oysters and oyster liquor
1 clove garlic, cut
1 T. margarine
½ tsp. salt
½ tsp. dried parsley flakes
1 qt. 2% milk
Dash of pepper
Paprika

Examine oysters carefully; remove all shells. Save oyster liquor after draining oysters. Rub a 2–quart saucepan with cut garlic. Add margarine, salt and parsley; heat until margarine melts. Add oysters and oyster liquor. Cook over medium heat until edges of oysters curl (do not overcook or oysters will be tough). Add milk and cook over low heat, stirring until very hot but not boiling. Add pepper. Serve garnished with paprika.

The old rule that says never eat oysters in a month without an "r" is no longer applicable, since they can quickly be refrigerated after harvesting. However, oysters do tend to be more watery and less meaty during "r–less" months, since that's when they spawn.

Southwestern Stew

1 T. oil

2 lbs. boneless pork shoulder or sirloin cubes, cut into 1½-inch cubes

2 c. onion, chopped

1 c. green pepper, chopped

2 garlic cloves, minced

2–3 T. chili powder

2 tsp. dried whole oregano leaves

¼ tsp. salt

2 cans (14½ oz. each) low–sodium chicken broth

3 c. potatoes, peeled and cut into 1-inch cubes

1 pkg. (10 oz.) frozen corn

1 can (15 ½ oz.) garbanzo beans, drained

Yield:
8 servings

Serving Size:
1 ¼ cups

Preparation Time:
30 minutes

Cooking Time:
1¾ hours

Nutrient Analysis per serving:

Calories: 369
Fat: 12.8 gm
Cholesterol: 76 mg
Sodium: 384 mg

Heat oil in a large Dutch oven. Add pork and brown over medium–high heat; drain fat. Stir in onions, green pepper, seasonings and chicken broth. Cover; cook over medium–low heat for 50–60 minutes, or until pork is tender. Add potatoes, corn and beans. Cover and cook 20–30 minutes longer.

Note: This recipe can be prepared ahead to the point where the meat is cooked. It can safely be refrigerated for 1–2 days before completing the recipe by adding vegetables and finishing the cooking process.

To remove fat from soup, cover and chill it overnight or until the fat solidifies on the surface of the soup. Then, lift it off and discard it.

Velvet Corn Chowder

Yield:
  4 servings

Serving Size:
  1 cup

Preparation Time:
  15–20 minutes

Cooking Time:
  15–20 minutes

Nutrient Analysis per serving:

Calories: 96
Fat: 1.8 gm
Cholesterol: 3 mg
Sodium: 522 mg

2 cans (10½ oz. each) low–sodium chicken broth
2 egg whites
2 T. skim milk
1 can (8¾ oz.) cream–style corn
2 T. cold water
1 T. cornstarch
¼ c. lean ham, finely chopped
Paprika

Bring chicken broth to a boil over high heat. Beat egg whites and milk until frothy and set aside. Add corn to broth and bring to a boil; reduce heat. Mix water and cornstarch; add to soup, cook and stir until thickened. Turn off heat and add egg white; stir quickly once. Add the ham; garnish with paprika and serve immediately.

Cutting calorie intake is one way to shed pounds. Calorie output counts, too! The best approach is to decrease calories AND increase physical activity.

Savory Seven Bean Soup

Bags of this bean mixture with a copy of this recipe make a wonderful gift. (What else are you going to do with all those beans?)

2 c. bean mixture *(see below)*, **rinsed**
8 c. water
1 large onion, chopped
1 lb. lean ham, diced
1 can (10 oz.) diced tomatoes and green chilies (*Rotel*** brand)**
1 clove garlic, minced
1 can (16 oz.) whole tomatoes, undrained
Juice of 1 lemon

Bean Mixture should contain equal amounts of the following:

Green Split Peas
Yellow Split Peas
Red Beans
Black–eyed Peas
Pinto Beans
Great Northern Beans
Lentils

Combine 2 cups of bean mixture, water, onion and ham in a 5–quart crockpot; simmer on LOW setting for 6 hours, stirring occasionally. Add remaining ingredients and simmer for 1 hour more.

Yield:
10 servings
Serving Size:
1 ¼ cups
Preparation Time:
15 minutes
Cooking Time:
7 hours

Nutrient Analysis per serving:

Calories: 198
Fat: 2.6 gm
Cholesterol: 17 mg
Sodium: 767 mg

Beans are one of the best sources of both soluble and insoluble fiber. While soluble fiber may be helpful in reducing blood cholesterol levels, insoluble fiber is helpful in preventing and treating constipation.

Gringo Chili

Whip this recipe up in minutes when the mood for chili hits you.

Yield:
6 servings

Serving Size:
1 ¼ cup

Preparation Time:
10–15 minutes

Cooking Time:
15–20 minutes

Nutrient Analysis per serving:

Calories: 261
Fat: 4 gm
Cholesterol: 43 mg
Sodium: 400 mg

1 lb. ground turkey
1 medium onion, chopped
2 cloves garlic, minced
1 can (32 oz.) diced tomatoes, undrained
1 can (15 oz.) pinto or kidney beans, drained
1 can (6 oz.) tomato paste
½ c. green chili salsa
1 T. chili powder

In a large nonstick skillet, cook turkey, onion and garlic over medium heat until turkey loses its pink color; drain excess fat. Stir in remaining ingredients; bring to boil. Cover, reduce heat and simmer 15–20 minutes.

Boulder Black Bean Soup

The perfect supper after an awesome day of skiing!

2 tsp. olive oil
1 medium onion, chopped
3 cloves garlic, minced
1 tsp. dried whole oregano
1/2 tsp. dried whole thyme
1/2 tsp. cumin
1/4 tsp. cayenne pepper
3 c. canned black beans, rinsed and drained
3 c. low–sodium chicken broth
2 tomatoes, chopped
1/2 c. onion, chopped (optional)
1/2 c. reduced–fat Monterey Jack cheese, shredded (optional)

Yield:
8 servings

Serving Size:
1 cup

Preparation Time:
15 minutes

Cooking Time:
25–35 minutes

Nutrient Analysis per serving:

Calories: 141
Fat: 4.5 gm
Cholesterol: 0 mg
Sodium: 32 mg

Heat oil in a large saucepan over medium heat. Sauté onion and garlic until tender (about 5 minutes). Stir in oregano, thyme, cumin and pepper; cook one minute longer. Place half of beans in a blender and puree until smooth, adding chicken broth as needed to make a smooth puree. Add puree, remaining whole beans and broth to saucepan. Bring to a boil over medium heat then simmer uncovered for 20–30 minutes. Serve garnished with diced tomatoes and, if desired, onion and shredded cheese.

An easy way to lower the sodium in your favorite recipe is to rinse canned beans and vegetables with water before using.

Creamy Potato Soup

Yield:
4 servings

Serving Size:
1 cup

Preparation Time:
20 minutes

Cooking Time:
20 minutes

*Nutrient Analysis
per serving:*

Calories: 144
Fat: 2.8 gm
Cholesterol: 1 mg
Sodium: 91 mg

1 lb. (3 medium) potatoes, peeled and
    thinly sliced
1 ½ c. low–sodium chicken broth
1 c. skim milk
2 tsp. margarine
⅓ c. green onion, sliced
2 T. fresh parsley, chopped
½ tsp. celery seed
¼ tsp. dried whole tarragon
⅛ tsp. pepper
Salt to taste

Combine potatoes and broth in 2–quart
saucepan. Bring to a boil; cover and cook until
potatoes are tender (about 10 minutes). Cool
slightly. Pour into blender and blend until
smooth; return to saucepan. Stir in milk,
margarine, onions, parsley, celery seed, tarragon and pepper. Bring to a boil; stir in salt.
Serve warm or cold, thinned with a little
additional milk.

Winter Stew

Try this one as soon as the snow flies!

1 lb. ground beef
1 small head cabbage, cored and cut in small wedges
1 small onion, chopped
1 c. celery, sliced
1 c. carrots, sliced
1 c. zucchini, sliced
1 c. turnip, sliced
1 can (46 oz.) *V–8 Juice*
1 c. brown rice, barley or bulgur
Pepper, to taste

Brown ground beef; drain fat. Place in crockpot, top with vegetables, cover with *V–8 Juice* and season with pepper. Cook for 4–6 hours on low setting. Add rice, barley or bulgur and cook 1 hour longer or until grain is cooked (allow 1$^{1}/_{2}$ hours to cook if using rice).

Yield:
12 servings

Serving Size:
1 cup

Preparation Time:
15–20 minutes

Cooking Time:
4–6 hours

Nutrient Analysis per serving:

Calories: 184
Fat: 5.6 gm
Cholesterol: 28 mg
Sodium: 481 mg

Brown rice takes twice as long to cook as white rice. So if time is limited, try quick–cooking brown rice.

"No Hassle" Split Pea Soup

*Serve with cornbread and fruit for
a cold weather evening.*

Yield:
8 servings

Serving Size:
1 cup

Preparation Time:
20 minutes

Cooking Time:
6–10 hours

**Nutrient Analysis
per serving:**

Calories: 258
Fat: 2.7 gm
Cholesterol: 16 mg
Sodium: 557 mg

**1 lb. dry green split peas (soaked overnight
and drained)**

1 qt. water

³/₄ lb. lean ham, cubed

¹/₂ T. onion powder

¹/₄ tsp. pepper

¹/₂ c. celery, chopped

1 c. carrots, sliced

1 medium onion, chopped

1 bay leaf (optional)

Put all ingredients into a crockpot. Cover and
cook on LOW for 10–12 hours or on HIGH for
5–6 hours.

*Switching from bacon
to lean ham in recipes
saves 1,499 calories
and 148 grams of fat.
(12 oz. bacon equal
1,995 calories and
166.8 gm. fat; 12 oz.
lean ham equal 496
calories and 18.8 gm.
fat.)*

Skier's Vegetable Chili

With a food processor, this superb chili
is a cinch to prepare.

1 c. onion, chopped
1/2 c. green pepper, diced
2 T. olive oil
2 garlic cloves, minced
2 c. zucchini, chopped
1 c. carrot, chopped
2 cans (15 oz. each) pinto or kidney beans,
    rinsed and drained
2 cans (16 oz. each) diced tomatoes
2 T. chili powder
1/4 tsp. cumin
1 tsp. Italian seasoning
Pepper, to taste
1/2 c. water

Yield:
    8 servings
Serving Size:
    1 cup
Preparation Time:
    25 minutes
Cooking Time:
    1 hour

Nutrient Analysis
per serving:

Calories: 227
Fat: 4.7 gm
Cholesterol: 0 mg
Sodium: 213 mg

In a 4–quart saucepan, sauté onion and green pepper in olive oil over medium–low heat until onions are soft (about 8 minutes). Add garlic; stir in zucchini and carrot. Cook over low heat for 2 minutes. To vegetable mixture add beans, tomatoes, chili powder, cumin, Italian seasoning, pepper and water; stir. Bring mixture to a boil; reduce heat and simmer for about 35–45 minutes.

Broccoli–Chicken Soup

*Keep these ingredients around for
surprise lunch guests.*

Yield:
    5 ½ cups
    4 servings

Serving Size:
    1 ⅓ cups

Preparation Time:
    5 minutes

Cooking Time:
    10 minutes

1 pkg. (10 oz.) frozen chopped broccoli
1 ½ c. water
2 cans (10¾ oz. each) 99% fat–free
    cream of chicken soup
1 c. skim milk
⅛ tsp. cayenne pepper (optional)
¼ c. Parmesan cheese

Cook broccoli in water until tender. Stir in soup,
milk and pepper; cook until thoroughly heated.
Serve topped with 1 tablespoon Parmesan
cheese.

**Nutrient Analysis
per serving:**

Calories: 196
Fat: 1.7 gm
Cholesterol: 4 mg
Sodium: 823 mg

Glenwood Gazpacho

*This delicious cool soup will remind you
of a refreshing dip in the famous
Glenwood Springs Hot Springs Pool.*

3 large tomatoes, chopped
1 bell pepper, chopped
1 cucumber, peeled and chopped
1 c. celery, chopped
1/2 c. onion, chopped
4 c. *V–8* or tomato juice
5 T. red wine vinegar
1/2 tsp. pepper

Combine all ingredients in a large non–metallic
bowl. Chill overnight.

Yield:
   8 servings

Serving Size:
   1 cup

Preparation Time:
   20 minutes

**Nutrient Analysis
per serving:**

Calories: 54
Fat: .4 gm
Cholesterol: 0 mg
Sodium: 467 mg

*The sodium content
of this soup can be
lowered by using two
cups low–sodium
V–8 Juice and two
cups regular
V–8 Juice.*

Chilled Cucumber–Herb Soup

Yield:
4 servings

Serving Size:
²/₃ cup

Preparation Time:
10 minutes

Chilling Time:
1 hour

**Nutrient Analysis
per serving:**

Calories: 56
Fat: .8 gm
Cholesterol: 2 mg
Sodium: 247 mg

1 large cucumber
1 c. low–fat buttermilk
1/2 c. low-fat plain yogurt
2 T. tarragon vinegar
2 clove garlic, minced
1 tsp. Dijon mustard
3 leaves fresh basil, chopped
¹/₄ tsp. dried whole tarragon
Salt and white pepper to taste

Scrub cucumber to remove any wax, but do not peel. Coarsely grate cucumber and drain. In a large bowl combine cucumber and remaining ingredients. Chill to allow flavors to blend. Serve garnished with a sprig of parsley.

If you think of soup only as something to warm you on those cold winter days, remember cold soups make great quick and healthy meals for days when the mercury is on the rise.

SALADS

SALADS

MAIN DISH SALADS

Breckenridge Broccoli Salad

A hit at potlucks!

3 c. broccoli flowerets

$^1/_2$ c. sharp reduced–fat Cheddar cheese, grated

$^1/_2$ c. red onion, sliced

3 T. bacon bits

<u>DRESSING:</u>

$^3/_4$ c. fat–free mayonnaise

3 T. sugar

1 $^1/_2$ T. vinegar

Combine broccoli, cheese, onion and bacon bits. Mix mayonnaise, sugar and vinegar and toss with broccoli mixture. Chill and serve.

Yield:
3 cups
6 servings

Serving Size:
$^1/_2$ cup

Preparation Time:
15 minutes

Nutrient Analysis per serving:

Calories: 101
Fat: 2.4 gm
Cholesterol: 0 mg
Sodium: 441 mg

A serving of broccoli (about one cup) contains more vitamin C than an orange — more than enough to meet the Recommended Dietary Allowance for one day.

Miner's Corn and Kidney Bean Salad

For a casual meal, serve this with Rancher's Meatloaf.

Yield:
5 cups
10 servings

Serving Size:
½ cup

Preparation Time:
10–15 minutes

Cooking Time:
5 minutes

Marinating Time:
8 hours

Nutrient Analysis per serving:

Calories: 119
Fat: .6 gm
Cholesterol: 0 mg
Sodium: 306 mg

2 cans (15 oz.) red kidney beans
1 ½ c. frozen corn, thawed
½ c. onion, finely chopped
½ c. green pepper, chopped
⅔ c. white wine vinegar
⅓ c. water
¼ c. sugar
⅛ tsp. cayenne pepper
1 tsp. celery seed

Drain and rinse kidney beans. In a medium bowl, combine kidney beans, corn, onion and green peppers; set aside. In a small saucepan, bring vinegar, water, sugar and red pepper to a boil; cook 1 minute. Remove from heat and stir in celery seed. Pour over vegetable mixture; toss gently. Cover and refrigerate for 8 hours, stirring occasionally.

Ounce for ounce, kidney beans have three times more fiber than green beans, and corn has about one and one-half times more.

66

Ramen Slaw

*Even if you don't like cabbage,
you'll enjoy this slaw.*

3 c. cabbage, shredded

4 green onions, sliced

2 tsp. sesame seeds

1 pkg. low–fat chicken–flavored Ramen
noodles, crumbled dry (reserve seasoning
packet)

$1/4$ c. water

3 T. sugar

2 T. oil

1 T. vinegar

$1/3$ c. slivered almonds, toasted (optional)

Toss cabbage, onion, sesame seeds, and dry
Ramen noodles together; set aside. Mix water,
sugar, oil, vinegar and Ramen seasoning to make
dressing. Pour dressing over cabbage mixture;
toss. Sprinkle with almonds (optional).

Yield:
　3 cups
　6 servings

Serving Size:
　$1/2$ cup

Preparation Time:
　15 minutes

*Nutrient Analysis
per serving:*

Calories:　　125
Fat:　　　　5.3 gm
Cholesterol:　0 mg
Sodium:　　179 mg

*Air–dried noodles
such as Campbell's
Lowfat Ramen
Noodles are lower in
fat than traditional
fried Ramen noodles.*

Chili Cheese Salad

*Cottage cheese lovers will love
this spicy modification.*

Yield:
    4 servings
Serving Size:
    ¹/₂ cup
Preparation Time:
    10 minutes

**1 container (15 oz.) 1% cottage cheese,
    drained**
1 can (7 oz.) chopped green chilies, drained
2 fresh tomatoes, cut into wedges
2 T. oil–free Italian dressing

Combine cottage cheese, tomatoes and chilies.
Pour dressing over mixture and toss. Chill.

**Nutrient Analysis
per serving:**

Calories: 104
Fat: 1.2 gm
Cholesterol: 4 mg
Sodium: 646 mg

Hint: Holds overnight very well; just toss again
before serving.

*Cottage cheese is an
excellent source of
protein. Just ¹/₂ cup
of lowfat cottage
cheese provides
one–third of your
protein needs for
the day.*

Carrot–Raisin Salad with Orange Yogurt Dressing

A delicious, nutrient–packed salad that will soon become a family favorite.

2 c. carrots, grated
⅔ c. raisins
¼ c. peach or orange flavored lowfat yogurt
2 T. frozen orange juice concentrate

Combine carrots and raisins; set aside. Blend yogurt and orange juice concentrate. Combine salad and dressing; mix well.

Yield:
   3 cups
   6 servings

Serving Size:
   ½ cup

Preparation Time:
   10 minutes

Nutrient Analysis per serving:

Calories: 81
Fat: .2 gm
Cholesterol: 0 mg
Sodium: 19 mg

When carrots and celery become limp, soak them in ice water. This will return some of the lost crispness by rehydrating cells that have lost water during storage.

Supreme Spinach Salad

*Pecans add a delicious crunch
to this spinach salad.*

Yield:
10 servings

Serving Size:
1 cup

Preparation Time:
15 minutes

**Nutrient Analysis
per serving:**

Calories: 124
Fat: 4.2 gm
Cholesterol: 2 mg
Sodium: 291 mg

1 bunch (10 oz.) fresh spinach
$\frac{1}{2}$ c. pecans, chopped
12 oz. 1% cottage cheese, rinsed with cold water and drained
1 c. plain nonfat yogurt
$\frac{1}{2}$ c. sugar
3 T. vinegar
1 tsp. dry mustard
1 T. prepared horseradish
$\frac{1}{2}$ tsp. salt

Wash spinach and refrigerate until crisp; tear into bite–sized pieces. Combine spinach, pecans and cottage cheese; mix lightly. Set aside. Combine yogurt, sugar, vinegar, mustard, horseradish and salt; mix well. Combine yogurt mixture and spinach mixture; toss lightly.

While Popeye promotes spinach as a good source of iron, it occurs in a form that is not well–absorbed by the body as is the iron in meat. However, eating iron–containing plant foods (e.g., spinach and grains) with a food rich in vitamin C increases the amount of iron the body can absorb.

70

Warm Broccoli Potato Salad

*A nice diversion from mayonnaise–laden
potato salad.*

6 medium new potatoes (about 2 lbs.),
   cut into 1-inch cubes
1 ½ to 2 c. fresh broccoli flowerets
¼ c. orange juice
2 T. olive oil
3 T. white wine vinegar
2 tsp. dried whole basil
1 large clove garlic, minced
¼ tsp. hot pepper sauce
2 T. fresh parsley, chopped
2 green onions, sliced
Salt, to taste

Cook potatoes, covered, in 1 inch of boiling water *just* until tender, 15–20 minutes. Drain; keep warm. Meanwhile, blanch broccoli in boiling water one minute; drain. Combine broccoli and potatoes; set aside. In small saucepan, combine juice, oil, vinegar, basil and garlic; bring to a boil. Remove from heat. Stir in pepper sauce; pour over potatoes and broccoli. Add parsley and onions; toss to coat. Add salt and toss. Serve warm.

Yield:
  4 cups
  8 servings
Serving Size:
  ½ cup
Preparation Time:
  15 minutes
Cooking Time:
  20 minutes

**Nutrient Analysis
per serving:**

Calories: 151
Fat: 3.8 gm
Cholesterol: 0 mg
Sodium: 105 mg

Traditional potato salad made with mayonnaise attributes over 50% of its calories to fat and about 85 mg of cholesterol. In this healthy potato salad recipe, only 32% of the calories come from fat and there is no cholesterol.

Spinach in a Mold

It takes a bit more effort, but the results are impressive — especially for a holiday dinner.

Yield:
8 servings

Serving Size:
$^1/_2$ cup

Preparation Time:
30 minutes

Chilling Time:
1–2 hours

Nutrient Analysis per serving:

Calories: 73
Fat: .3 gm
Cholesterol: 1 mg
Sodium: 293 mg

1 pkg. (3 oz.) lemon Jello
1 $^3/_4$ c. water, divided
1 $^1/_2$ T. vinegar
$^1/_2$ c. fat–free mayonnaise
$^1/_4$ tsp. salt
1 tsp. prepared horseradish
$^1/_3$ c. celery, chopped
1 T. onion, minced
1 c. frozen chopped spinach, thawed
  and drained
$^3/_4$ c. 1% cottage cheese

In a large mixing bowl, dissolve Jello in $^3/_4$ cup boiling water. Add 1 cup cold water, vinegar, mayonnaise, horseradish and salt. Put in freezer; chill until firm 1 inch around sides of bowl. Remove from freezer; beat with an electric mixer until fluffy. Add celery, onion, spinach and cottage cheese. Place in 1–quart mold and chill in refrigerator until firm. (Best done a day ahead.)

Hint: Use pimiento strips to form poinsettia leaf flowers at holiday time; sliced black or green stuffed olives can be used to garnish unmolded salad, as well as radish slices.

When making molded salads, you'll find that the mold will come easily out of the pan if you spray it with nonstick cooking spray before filling.

Jicama and Orange Salad

*Served on a lettuce leaf, this makes
a beautiful, refreshing salad.*

**1 can (11 oz.) mandarin orange segments,
    drained**
2 c. jicama, julienne-cut
2 T. orange juice
2 T. rice vinegar
1 tsp. olive oil

Combine oranges and jicama in a medium bowl.
Mix together juice, vinegar and oil. Pour
dressing over orange/jicama mixture and chill.

Yield:
    6 servings
Serving Size:
    $^1/_2$ cup
Preparation Time:
    5 minutes

*Nutrient Analysis
per serving:*

Calories: 45
Fat: .8 gm
Cholesterol: 0 mg
Sodium: 5 mg

*Jicama is a tropical
root vegetable that
resembles a giant
turnip. The taste
and texture is a cross
between an apple and
a water chestnut.*

Saucy Fruit Salad

This jazzy fruit salad is great to take for potlucks.

Yield:
5 cups
10 servings

Serving Size:
½ cup

Preparation Time:
20–25 minutes

Nutrient Analysis per serving:

Calories: 144
Fat: .6 gm
Cholesterol: 1 mg
Sodium: 41 mg

1 can (11 oz.) mandarin oranges, drained
1 can (20 oz.) pineapple chunks, drained
3 bananas, sliced
2 red apples, chopped

FRUIT SAUCE:

1 box (1.3 oz.) sugar–free instant
  vanilla pudding
1 c. skim milk
⅓ c. orange juice concentrate
1 carton (6 oz.) low–fat banana yogurt

Mix all fruit and set aside. Combine dry pudding with milk, orange juice and banana yogurt, beat with wire whisk until smooth. Combine fruit and sauce. Chill. Serve garnished with fruit.

By leaving the skin on apples rather than peeling and discarding them, you can significantly increase your fiber intake.

74

Confetti Pasta Salad

Double this recipe for your next party!

**2 c. dry eggless corkscrew pasta, cooked
and drained**

1 ½ c. mushrooms, sliced

1 c. cherry tomatoes, halved

1 c. zucchini, sliced

**1 can (14 oz.) quartered artichoke hearts,
drained**

¼ c. green onions, sliced

⅔ c. oil–free Italian dressing

3 T. Parmesan cheese, grated

In a large bowl, combine pasta and vegetables; cover with Italian dressing and marinate in refrigerator for several hours. Drain. Sprinkle cheese over pasta/vegetable mixture; toss lightly. Chill and serve.

Yield:
6 servings

Serving Size:
½ cup

Preparation Time:
20 minutes

Marinating Time:
1–2 hours

**Nutrient Analysis
per serving:**

Calories: 138
Fat: 1.2 gm
Cholesterol: 2 mg
Sodium: 46 mg

Most Americans don't consume enough complex carbohy-drates (starchy foods) to promote optimal health. One way to increase your intake is to eat pasta for meals at least three times per week, using different low–fat sauces for variety.

75

Tempting Tortellini Salad

Double this recipe — it's great for lunch the next day.

Yield:
10 servings

Serving Size:
¹/₂ cup

Preparation Time:
15 minutes

Cooking Time:
10 minutes

Nutrient Analysis per serving:

Calories: 105
Fat: 3.5 gm
Cholesterol: 4 mg
Sodium: 116 mg

1 pkg. (9 oz.) refrigerated cheese tortellini or frozen tortellini

2 c. fresh, ripe tomatoes

3 large leaves of fresh basil

3 sprigs of fresh parsley

2 cloves garlic, minced

1 ¹/₂ T. olive oil

2 tsp. red wine vinegar

¹/₄ tsp. salt

¹/₄ tsp. freshly ground pepper

Cook tortellini according to package directions until tender. Meanwhile, dice tomatoes in ¹/₄-inch pieces; place in large bowl. Finely chop basil and parsley. Add herbs and garlic to tomatoes. Gently stir in oil, vinegar, salt and pepper. Drain tortellini and toss with tomato mixture to coat.

The only pasta that contains cholesterol is egg noodles. One cup of egg noodles supplies about 70 mg. of cholesterol.

Sweet & Sour Pasta Salad

A tangy side dish, or add chicken for a main dish salad.

1 ⅓ c. eggless corkscrew pasta, uncooked
1 can (15 oz.) unsweetened pineapple chunks, drained
2 c. broccoli flowerets
1 c. celery, chopped
1 c. frozen petite peas
½ c. sweet red pepper, chopped
¼ c. green onion, sliced

DRESSING:

⅓ c. white wine vinegar
2 T. Dijon mustard
2 T. honey
2 T. lemon juice
2 T. canned pineapple juice
1 T. olive oil
½ tsp. dried whole basil
½ tsp. garlic powder

Yield:
 10 servings
Serving Size:
 1 cup
Preparation Time:
 20 minutes

*Nutrient Analysis
per serving:*

Calories: 145
Fat: 2.2 gm
Cholesterol: 0 mg
Sodium: 76 mg

Cook pasta according to package directions. Drain pineapple chunks; reserve 2 tablespoons of juice for dressing. Mix dressing ingredients together. Combine all salad ingredients and toss with dressing. Chill, then serve.

Uncooked pasta of similar sizes and shape may be interchanged in recipes, but measure by weight and not volume.

Garden Pasta Salad

Yield:
12 servings

Serving Size:
1/2 cup

Preparation Time:
30 minutes

Standing Time:
2 hours

Cooking Time:
10 minutes

**1 pkg. (8–10 oz.) eggless corkscrew
pasta noodles, uncooked**
3 carrots, sliced and quartered
1 cucumber, peeled and diced
6–8 radishes, topped and sliced
1 c. broccoli flowerets
**2 pkgs. dry Good Seasons low–cal
Italian dressing**
1/2 c. vinegar
1/4 c. water
Parmesan cheese, grated

*Nutrient Analysis
per serving:*

Calories: 111
Fat: .6 gm
Cholesterol: 1 mg
Sodium: 195 mg

Cook noodles according to package directions. Rinse under cold running water and drain; place in large bowl. Add cut vegetables; mix well. Prepare dressing using two packages of dry Good Seasons dressing mix, vinegar and water; mix well. Pour dressing over salad. Let set in refrigerator for approximately 2 hours. Mix prior to serving and garnish with Parmesan cheese.

Using tri–colored pasta in recipes is a colorful, easy way to make pasta dishes look festive. The colors are derived from plant dyes and usually do not change the flavor or nutritive content of the pasta.

Broadmoor Chicken Salad

Spinach salad lovers — this is for you!

DRESSING:

1/3 c. cider vinegar

3 T. water

1 T. oil

2 T. brown sugar

2 T. green onion, sliced

2 tsp. Dijon mustard

1/2 tsp. salt

1/4 tsp. pepper

SALAD:

3 bunches fresh spinach, torn

1 1/2 c. cooked chicken, cubed and chilled

1/2 lb. mushrooms, sliced

1 small avocado, peeled and sliced

1 1/2 c. alfalfa sprouts

1/4 c. green onion, sliced

1 can (8 oz.) sliced water chestnuts, drained

Yield:
　4 servings

Serving Size:
　1 1/2 cups

Preparation Time:
　35 minutes

*Nutrient Analysis
per serving:*

Calories:　　326
Fat:　　　　14 gm
Cholesterol:　38 mg
Sodium:　　　649 mg

Combine dressing ingredients in a jar; shake vigorously. Chill at least 30 minutes. Toss together spinach, chicken, mushrooms, avocado, sprouts, green onion and water chestnuts. Serve drizzled with dressing.

*An easy way to wash spinach leaves is to immerse them in **warm** water to help loosen sand and dirt. Rinse with **cold** water to freshen/revive the leaves.*

Oriental Salad

*Keep cooked chicken on hand
for this unique salad.*

Yield:
6 servings

Serving Size:
1 ¹/₂ cups

Preparation Time:
10 minutes

Cooking Time:
10 minutes

**Nutrient Analysis
per serving:**

Calories: 234
Fat: 9 gm
Cholesterol: 68 mg
Sodium: 353 mg

DRESSING:

³/₄ c. white wine vinegar

¹/₄ cup sugar

1 tsp. sesame oil

1 tsp. oil

¹/₂ tsp. salt

¹/₄ tsp. pepper

SALAD:

3 c. (about 1 lb.) cooked chicken, cubed

1 large head Romaine lettuce, shredded

¹/₃ c. celery, diced

3 green onions, sliced

1 can (11 oz.) mandarin oranges, drained

1 c. chow mein noodles

Combine vinegar, sugar, oils, salt and pepper in a small saucepan. Heat until sugar is dissolved, stirring frequently. Set aside to cool. Toss chicken, lettuce, celery and onion with cooled dressing. Top with mandarin oranges and chow mein noodles.

Salad greens will keep up to two weeks if stored properly in the refrigerator. Before refrigerating, wash lettuce and let drain; while still damp, roll the lettuce up in paper towels and place it in a plastic bag. Fresh herbs also keep longer when stored in this manner.

Spinach Salad with Fruit and Beef

Pleasing to the eye and the palate.

1 lb. beef top round steak
$\frac{1}{2}$ c. white wine vinegar
$\frac{1}{4}$ c. Worcestershire sauce
$\frac{1}{4}$ c. onion, finely chopped
2 T. sesame seeds
1 $\frac{1}{2}$ T. sugar
4 cloves garlic, minced
2 tsp. chili powder
$\frac{1}{2}$ tsp. white pepper
2 T. oil
1 bunch fresh spinach leaves, washed and torn
2 medium oranges, peeled and sectioned
2 c. fresh strawberries, sliced

Yield:
4 servings
Serving Size:
1 salad
Preparation Time:
20 minutes
Cooking Time:
15–20 minutes

Nutrient Analysis per serving:

Calories:	309
Fat:	12 gm
Cholesterol:	69 mg
Sodium:	225 mg

Trim excess fat from steak. Broil 6 inches from heat, 6–7 minutes per side for rare or until desired doneness. Slice steak diagonally across the grain into thin slices; place in glass baking dish to keep warm; set aside. Place vinegar, Worcestershire sauce, onion, sesame seeds, sugar, garlic, chili powder and white pepper in blender; cover. Process until blended. Gradually add oil while blender is running. Pour half of sauce over steak slices and cover; chill remaining sauce. Refrigerate steak at least 3 hours, but no longer than 24 hours. Place spinach on serving plates. Arrange beef slices, orange and strawberry slices on spinach. Serve drizzled with remaining sauce.

Asparagus Salmon Salad

Attractive salad that's ready in minutes.

Yield:
2 servings

Serving Size:
1 salad

Preparation Time:
20 minutes

Cooking Time:
3–5 minutes

***Nutrient Analysis
per serving:***

Calories: 280
Fat: 12 gm
Cholesterol: 36 mg
Sodium: 708 mg

1 T. olive oil
½ c. rice vinegar
1 tsp. Dijon mustard
¼ tsp. dried whole thyme
¼ tsp. salt
¾ lb. fresh or frozen whole asparagus
1 can (6¾ oz.) salmon, drained and flaked
    OR leftover salmon
Lettuce leaves
2 tomatoes, cut in wedges
Freshly ground pepper

Combine oil, vinegar, mustard, thyme and salt in a jar; shake vigorously. Chill. Steam asparagus until tender (about 3–5 minutes); cool. Line salad plates with lettuce leaves. Arrange asparagus spears, salmon and tomato wedges on lettuce. Drizzle dressing over top; season with pepper and serve.

Snowmass Shrimp Louis

*As refreshing as the cool mountain
air of Snowmass.*

2 c. small frozen cooked shrimp, peeled
  and thawed
1 pkg. (10 oz.) frozen peas, thawed
1/4 c. red onion, chopped
DRESSING:
1/2 c. plain nonfat yogurt
2 T. light mayonnaise
1 tsp. dried dillweed

In a medium bowl, combine shrimp, peas and
onion. In a separate bowl, blend yogurt,
mayonnaise and dillweed. Toss shrimp mixture
with dressing. Chill for 30 minutes to blend
flavors, then serve in a lettuce cup.

Yield:
  4 servings
Serving Size:
  2/3 cup
Preparation Time:
  15 minutes

*Nutrient Analysis
per serving:*

Calories: 144
Fat: 2.7 gm
Cholesterol: 87 mg
Sodium: 218 mg

*Fortunately, salt
water seafood is
generally no higher
in sodium than fresh
water seafood*

Quick Taco Salad

*Keep these ingredients on hand for a light
Mexican dinner after a busy day.*

Yield:
  4 servings

Serving Size:
  1 salad

Preparation Time:
  10 minutes

Cooking Time:
  15–20 minutes

**Nutrient Analysis
per serving:**

Calories: 375
Fat: 12 gm
Cholesterol: 0 mg
Sodium: 916 mg

8 corn tortillas

Water

**1 can (15 oz.) beans with tomatoes, peppers
  and Mexican spices**

6 c. lettuce, shredded

**½ c. (2 oz.) sharp reduced–fat Cheddar
  cheese, shredded**

1 small avocado

1 large tomato, chopped

Preheat oven to 350°. Dip tortillas in water;
drain on paper towels. Cut each tortilla into 8
wedges and place on ungreased baking sheet.
Bake for 15 minutes or until crisp and golden.
Cool and set aside.

Place beans in a saucepan and heat thoroughly.
On a serving plate, layer lettuce, beans, cheese,
avocado and tomato. Place tortilla chips around
edge; serve with *Salsa Fresca* (page 201) or
commercial salsa.

Polynesian Chicken Salad

*Inspired by a mountain cafe in Aspen that serves
the best chicken salad — this is equally good.*

2 c. (8 oz.) cooked chicken breast, diced
³/₄ c. pineapple chunks, drained
¹/₂ c. celery, diced
¹/₄ c. slivered almonds, toasted
4 green onions, sliced
¹/₂ c. plain nonfat yogurt
¹/₄ c. fat–free mayonnaise
Romaine lettuce leaves

Combine chicken, pineapple, celery, almonds
and onions; set aside. Blend together yogurt and
mayonnaise; stir into chicken mixture. Serve on
a bed of lettuce.

Yield:
  4 servings

Serving Size:
  ³/₄ cup

Preparation Time:
  10 minutes

***Nutrient Analysis
per serving:***

Calories: 226
Fat: 6.6 gm
Cholesterol: 48 mg
Sodium: 253 mg

*Water chestnuts are
not nuts but tubers
(root vegetables).
Unlike nuts, they
are low in fat
and calories.*

Tuna on a Shoestring

The perfect dish for a potluck buffet.

Yield:
    4 servings

Serving Size:
    1 cup

Preparation Time:
    10 minutes

1 c. celery, chopped
1 c. carrots, grated
1 can (6 ½ oz.) tuna, packed in water, drained
¼ c. green onion, sliced
1 c. lettuce, shredded
¼ c. plain nonfat yogurt
¼ c. light mayonnaise
1 c. shoestring potatoes

Nutrient Analysis per serving:

Calories: 157
Fat: 5 gm
Cholesterol: 11 mg
Sodium: 303 mg

Toss together celery, carrots, tuna, onions and lettuce. Combine yogurt and mayonnaise for dressing. Just before serving, fold dressing and shoestring potatoes into tuna mixture.

Tuna packed in water retains its omega–3 fatty acids (the ones that protect against heart disease) and has less than half the calories of tuna packed in oil.

VEGETABLES

VEGETABLES

Grilled Potato Salad

*A unique compliment to grilled meats
that provides a pleasant alternative to
traditional potato salad.*

1 lb. small new potatoes, quartered
1 medium sweet red or green pepper, cubed
1 medium onion, sliced
1 T. olive oil
1 ½ tsp. dried whole rosemary
1 clove garlic, minced
⅛ tsp. crushed red pepper flakes (optional)
½ tsp. salt

Combine potatoes, pepper and onion in a large bowl; set aside. Heat oil, rosemary, garlic and pepper flakes together in a small saucepan. Remove from heat. Toss olive oil mixture with vegetables; sprinkle with salt. Place vegetables in a large square of heavy–duty aluminum foil; seal. Place foil package on grill over medium to hot coals. Cook for 45 minutes, turning once.

Yield:
4 cups
4 servings

Serving Size:
1 cup

Preparation Time:
10–15 minutes

Cooking Time:
45 minutes

*Nutrient Analysis
per serving:*

Calories: 140
Fat: 3.7 gm
Cholesterol: 0 mg
Sodium: 304 mg

*"Light" olive oil isn't
any lower in calories
or fat than regular
olive oil. It's just
milder in flavor.*

Sweet & Sour Carrots

1 lb. carrots, diagonally sliced
1 medium green pepper, cut into
bite–sized chunks
1 can (8 oz.) pineapple chunks (in own juice)
1/3 c. sugar
1 T. cornstarch
1/2 tsp. salt
2 T. cider vinegar
2 tsp. low–sodium soy sauce

Yield:
6 servings

Serving Size:
1/2 cup

Preparation Time:
15 minutes

Cooking Time:
20 minutes

Nutrient Analysis per serving:

Calories: 107
Fat: .2 gm
Cholesterol: 0 mg
Sodium: 340 mg

Cook carrots in boiling water until tender (10–15 minutes). Add green pepper and cook 3 minutes longer; drain and set aside. Drain pineapple juice into measuring cup; add water to measure 1/3 cup liquid. Reserve pineapple chunks. In a small saucepan, combine sugar, cornstarch and salt. Stir in pineapple liquid, vinegar and soy sauce until smooth. Stirring over medium heat, bring to a boil and simmer 1–2 minutes until thickened. Pour over carrots and green pepper; stir in pineapple. Serve hot or cold.

One of the benefits of eating carrots is that they contain carotene. In your body, carotene is converted into vitamin A and is thought to protect against some forms of cancer.

Riverside Picnic Vegetables

*Find a picnic spot on the banks of a
Colorado river and enjoy!*

4 to 5 medium potatoes (about 1$\frac{1}{2}$ lbs.)
$\frac{1}{2}$ c. red wine vinegar
2 T. water
2 T. oil
1 clove garlic, minced
1 tsp. dried whole basil
$\frac{1}{4}$ tsp. dried whole oregano
$\frac{1}{4}$ tsp. pepper
3 T. green onions, sliced
2 T. fresh parsley, chopped
Salt to taste
2 tomatoes, sliced
1 $\frac{1}{2}$ c. zucchini, shredded

Yield:
6 servings
Serving Size:
1 cup
Preparation Time:
15 minutes
Cooking Time:
30 minutes

*Nutrient Analysis
per serving:*

Calories: 159
Fat: 4.9 gm
Cholesterol: 0 mg
Sodium: 108 mg

In 2–quart saucepan, cook potatoes, covered, in
about 1 inch boiling water just until tender
(about 30 minutes). Meanwhile, prepare
dressing: combine vinegar, water, oil, garlic,
basil, oregano, pepper, onions, parsley and salt
in a jar; shake vigorously and chill. Drain, cool
and slice potatoes $\frac{1}{4}$-inch thick. In serving bowl,
layer half the potatoes, tomatoes and zucchini;
pour half the dressing over vegetables. Top with
remaining potatoes, tomatoes, zucchini and
dressing. Cover and chill.

Sesame Broccoli

Yield:
  6 servings
Serving Size:
  ²/₃ cup
Preparation Time:
  5 minutes
Cooking Time:
  6–10 minutes

**Nutrient Analysis
per serving:**

Calories: 28
Fat: .9 gm
Cholesterol: 0 mg
Sodium: 16 mg

4 c. broccoli flowerets
2 T. rice vinegar
1 T. water
¹/₂ tsp. sesame oil
1 tsp. lemon juice
¹/₂ tsp. ground ginger
1 tsp. sesame seed, toasted

Arrange broccoli in a vegetable steamer over boiling water. Cover and steam 6–10 minutes or until tender. Place in serving dish; set aside and keep warm. Combine vinegar, water, oil, ginger and lemon juice; pour over broccoli and toss to coat. Sprinkle with sesame seeds.

Rice vinegar is a sweet, mild vinegar that makes an excellent dressing combined with seasonings or all by itself — and it contains no fat!

92

Green Beans Telluride

Serve with Smokey Beef Brisket and hot rolls.

2 cans (16 oz each) uncut green beans
1 can (8 oz.) sliced water chestnuts, drained
Cooking spray
¼ c. green onion, sliced
½ c. low–fat sour cream
1 tsp. sugar
1 tsp. vinegar
Salt and pepper to taste

In a saucepan, heat beans. Add chestnuts and continue to heat 2 minutes. Meanwhile, in a small saucepan coated with cooking spray, sauté onions until tender. Stir remaining ingredients into onions. and warm over medium heat, don't boil. To serve, drain bean mixture and toss with sauce.

Yield:
  6 servings
Serving Size:
  ²/₂ cup
Preparation Time:
  5 minutes
Cooking Time:
  10 minutes

Nutrient Analysis per serving:

Calories: 80
Fat: 2.6 gm
Cholesterol: 8 mg
Sodium: 489 mg

93

Deli Carrots

A healthier version of mom's old favorite — Copper Pennies.

Yield:
    12 servings

Serving Size:
    $2/3$ cup

Preparation Time:
    10 minutes

Marinating Time:
    12 hours

**Nutrient Analysis
per serving:**

Calories: 120
Fat: 4 gm
Cholesterol: 0 mg
Sodium: 193 mg

5 c. fresh or frozen carrots, sliced
1 c. onion, thinly sliced
$1/2$ c. green pepper, chopped
1 can ($10^1/2$ oz.) tomato soup
3 T. oil
$2/3$ c. sugar
$2/3$ c. cider vinegar
1 tsp. dry mustard
1 tsp. Worcestershire sauce
1 tsp. seasoned pepper

Cook carrots until barely tender; drain and cool. Toss carrots with onion and green pepper. Combine remaining ingredients together and pour over vegetables; cover tightly. Marinate 12 hours. Serve cold. Carrots will keep for 2 weeks.

Note: Recipe can be cut in half for smaller groups. Then use the remaining half can of soup in other dishes or soups.

Microwaving vegetables is not only quick and convenient, but it helps retain the flavor and many of the nutrients found in vegetables.

Vail Vegetable Medley

1 large sweet red pepper
1 large sweet yellow pepper
2 large carrots, cut into strips
1 medium onion, chopped
2 cloves garlic, minced
1 tsp. olive oil
2 large zucchini, julienne cut
2 tsp. dried whole basil
1/2 tsp. salt
1/2 tsp. pepper

Yield:
  8 servings
Serving Size:
  1/2 cup
Preparation Time:
  10 minutes
Cooking Time:
  7 minutes

Seed red and yellow pepper and cut into 1/4-inch strips. Sauté peppers, carrots, onion and garlic in oil in a nonstick skillet for 5 minutes. Add zucchini strips and cook for 2 minutes or until vegetables are tender. Stir in basil, salt and pepper.

Nutrient Analysis
per serving:

Calories: 36
Fat: .8 gm
Cholesterol: 0 mg
Sodium: 159 mg

*Red peppers have
nearly four times
as much vitamin C
as oranges.*

Broccoli with Dill Cheese Sauce

Yield:
4 servings

Serving Size:
1 cup

Preparation Time:
8 minutes

Cooking Time:
2–5 minutes

4 c. broccoli flowerets
½ c. water
CHEESE SAUCE:
1 c. low–fat buttermilk
¼ c. Parmesan cheese, grated
1 tsp. Dijon mustard
2 tsp. cornstarch
1 tsp. dried dillweed

Place broccoli flowerets and water in a microwave safe dish. Cover dish with plastic wrap and microwave on HIGH power for 8–10 minutes or until tender. Meanwhile, combine buttermilk, Parmesan cheese, Dijon mustard and cornstarch in a small saucepan. Using a wire whisk, stir constantly until sauce boils. Cook over low heat for 2 minutes. Stir in dillweed and serve over drained broccoli.

Nutrient Analysis per serving:

Calories: 77
Fat: 2.2 gm
Cholesterol: 6 mg
Sodium: 184 mg

Cruciferous vegetables, such as Brussels sprouts, broccoli, cauliflower and cabbage, contain a substance that may protect the body against certain forms of cancer.

Garlic Squash on the Grill

Vegetables cook up beautifully on the grill.

1 clove garlic, minced
1 tsp. olive oil
2 tsp. water
1 tsp. dried whole basil
¼ tsp. lemon–pepper seasoning
¼ tsp. salt
2 medium zucchini, cut in half lengthwise
2 medium yellow squash, cut in half lengthwise

Combine garlic, oil, water and seasoning. Brush cut surfaces of squash with half of the garlic mixture. Place vegetables on clean, preheated grill, cut side down. Grill for 4 minutes, turn and brush with remaining garlic mixture. Cook for 4 more minutes or until tender.

Yield:
  4 servings

Serving Size:
  ½ medium squash

Preparation Time:
  3–5 minutes

Cooking Time:
  8 minutes

Nutrient Analysis per serving:

Calories: 33
Fat: 1.3 gm
Cholesterol: 0 mg
Sodium: 150 mg

Monounsaturated fats such as canola oil and olive oil can help lower blood cholesterol levels. However, they still contain the same number of calories as any other oil — 120 calories per tablespoon!

Grilled Corn–on–the–Cob

4 ears fresh corn
Butter–flavored cooking spray
1/2 tsp. lemon–pepper seasoning

Remove husks and silks from corn just before grilling. Coat each ear with cooking spray and sprinkle with lemon–pepper seasoning. Place each ear on a piece of heavy–duty aluminum foil and roll up; twist foil at each end. Grill, covered, over medium–hot coals for 20 minutes, turning occasionally.

Yield:
  4 servings

Serving Size:
  1 ear

Preparation Time:
  5 minutes

Cooking Time:
  20 minutes

Nutrient Analysis per serving:

Calories: 123
Fat: .9 gm
Cholesterol: 0 mg
Sodium: 6 mg

Eat fresh corn as soon as possible for the best sweet flavor. A chemical reaction converts the sugar in corn into starch after it is picked. For this reason, old corn won't be as sweet and delicious.

Skinny Oven Fries

Oh so satisfying when the urge for French fries begins to overwhelm you.

2 tsp. Parmesan cheese, grated
1 tsp. salt
1 tsp. sugar
1/2 tsp. garlic powder
1/2 tsp. paprika
1/4 tsp. onion powder
1/4 tsp. chili powder
1/4 tsp. lemon–pepper seasoning
4 large potatoes
1 T. olive oil
1 T. water

Yield:
   32 wedges
   8 servings

Serving Size:
   4 wedges

Preparation Time:
   5–10 minutes

Cooking Time:
   45–60 minutes

Preheat oven to 350°. Mix seasonings. Cut each potato into 8 wedges. Combine oil and water. Brush wedges with oil and water mixture and place on baking sheet. Sprinkle potatoes with seasoning mixture. Bake until soft when pricked with a fork, about 45 minutes. For crisp fries, bake 1 hour.

Nutrient Analysis per serving:

Calories: 86
Fat: 1.9 gm
Cholesterol: 0 mg
Sodium: 309 mg

Which would you choose: our Skinny Oven Fries or a small order of fast food French fries at 220 calories and 11.5 grams of fat?

Skillet Zucchini Pancake

A great recipe for a bumper zucchini crop!

Yield:
4 servings

Serving Size:
¼ of pancake

Preparation Time:
15 minutes

Cooking Time:
14–18 minutes

**Nutrient Analysis
per serving:**

Calories: 97
Fat: 3.4 gm
Cholesterol: 46 mg
Sodium: 158 mg

2 c. zucchini, grated and squeezed dry
¾ c. potato, peeled, grated and squeezed dry
¼ c. green onions, sliced
2 T. flour
1 egg, beaten
2 egg whites
1 clove garlic, crushed
Salt and pepper, to taste
2 tsp. margarine, divided
1 T. Parmesan cheese, grated

In a medium bowl, combine zucchini, potato, green onions, flour, egg, egg whites, garlic, salt and pepper. Melt 1 teaspoon margarine in a nonstick skillet over moderate heat, making sure bottom and sides of pan are well coated. Add zucchini mixture, shaping it into a cake with a spatula; cook uncovered over medium heat until golden around the edges (8–10 minutes). Place a large plate over the skillet and invert the pancake onto it. Add the remaining margarine to the skillet; melt over moderate heat. Slide the pancake back into the skillet and cook uncovered until firm (about 6–8 minutes). Sprinkle with Parmesan cheese.

Tangy Mashed Potatoes

A marvelous way to serve mashed potatoes without drizzling gravy all over them.

2 lbs. potatoes, peeled and cut into ³/₄-inch pieces
1 c. plain nonfat yogurt
¹/₄ c. green onion, sliced
1 T. margarine

Place potatoes in boiling water and cook until tender (about 20 minutes); drain. In a bowl, combine potatoes, yogurt and margarine. Beat with electric mixer until fluffy. Stir in green onion; season with salt and pepper to taste. Serve hot.

Yield:
6 servings
Serving Size:
²/₃ cup
Preparation Time:
10 minutes
Cooking Time:
20 minutes

Nutrient Analysis per serving:

Calories: 152
Fat: 2 gm
Cholesterol: 0 mg
Sodium: 51 mg

Bananas are often recommended as a high potassium food, but potatoes actually contain twice as much.

Ranch Potato Topper

Your family will love this — just don't tell them it's lowfat!

Yield:
　4 servings

Serving Size:
　¼ cup

Preparation Time:
　5 minutes

8 oz. 1 % cottage cheese
2 T. skim milk
1 tsp. dry Ranch Dressing mix
2 T. green onions, sliced
1 T. bacon bits

In a blender combine cottage cheese, milk and Ranch Dressing mix. Process 1–2 minutes or until smooth. Stir in onions and bacon bits. Serve on baked potatoes in place of sour cream.

Nutrient Analysis per serving:

Calories:　　56
Fat:　　　　1.7 gm
Cholesterol:　2 mg
Sodium:　　 376 mg

When eating in a restaurant, remember that you're in control. Don't hesitate to ask for items to be broiled or grilled instead of fried, and for salad dressings and potato toppings "on the side."

102

Spaghetti Squash Marinara

A truly fun vegetable!

1 medium spaghetti squash (about 3 to 3½ lbs.)
3 c. commercial low–fat spaghetti or
  marinara sauce
¼ c. Parmesan cheese, grated

Cut spaghetti squash in half length-wise and remove seeds. Place squash halves, cut side down, in a large glass baking dish. Cover dish with plastic wrap and microwave on HIGH for 8–10 minutes or until tender. Drain squash. Using a fork, remove spaghetti–like strands of squash. Warm spaghetti sauce over medium heat. Portion spaghetti squash on plates, top with sauce, then sprinkle evenly with cheese.

Yield:
  6 servings

Serving Size:
  1 cup

Preparation Time:
  5 minutes

Cooking Time:
  1 hour

**Nutrient Analysis
per serving:**

Calories: 213
Fat: 83 gm
Cholesterol: 4 mg
Sodium: 375 mg

103

Spaghetti squash is a yellow, football–shaped vegetable with pale yellow, stringy meat that resembles spaghetti when it is cooked.

Roaring Fork Ratatouille

Yield:
6 servings

Serving Size:
1 cup

Preparation Time:
20 minutes

Cooking Time:
30 minutes

Nutrient Analysis per serving:

Calories: 47
Fat: .4 gm
Cholesterol: 0 mg
Sodium: 405 mg

Cooking spray
1 medium onion, chopped
4 cloves garlic, crushed
1 small eggplant, peeled and cubed
2 medium bell peppers, cut into strips
1 c. tomato juice
3 T. dry red wine
1 bay leaf
1 tsp. dried whole basil
1 tsp. dried whole marjoram
$\frac{1}{2}$ tsp. dried whole oregano
1 tsp. salt
1 medium zucchini, sliced
2 medium tomatoes, cut in chunks
$\frac{1}{2}$ c. water (if needed)

Coat a large, Dutch oven with cooking spray. Add onion and garlic; sauté until tender (about 5 minutes). Add eggplant, peppers, tomato juice, wine and seasonings; mix well. Cover and simmer until vegetables are tender (about 10-15 minutes). Add zucchini and tomatoes, cover and simmer 10 more minutes or until all vegetables are tender. (Add water as needed.) Serve as a hearty vegetable stew or on a bed of rice.

Since preventing moisture loss in vegetables is important in maintaining quality and freshness, some vegetables are coated with a harmless wax to reduce moisture loss.

BREADS

BREADS

MUFFINS

Cranberry Nut Bread

2 c. flour
¾ c. sugar
1 ½ tsp. baking powder
½ tsp. baking soda
½ tsp. salt
¾ c. orange juice
2 T. oil
1 egg
1 ½ c. fresh cranberries, coarsely chopped
⅓ c. walnuts, chopped
1 T. grated orange peel
Cooking spray

Yield:
 1 loaf
 12 slices

Serving Size:
 1 slice

Preparation Time:
 20–25 minutes

Cooking Time:
 65–75 minutes

Preheat oven to 350°. In a large bowl, combine flour, sugar, baking powder, baking soda and salt. In a medium bowl, beat together orange juice, oil and egg until blended. Stir juice mixture into flour mixture just until moistened. Gently stir in cranberries, walnuts and orange peel. Spoon batter evenly into an 8½ x 4½ x 2½-inch loaf pan coated with cooking spray. Bake 65–75 minutes or until a wooden pick inserted into the center comes out clean. Cool bread in pan for 10 minutes, then remove from pan and cool on wire rack.

Nutrient Analysis
per serving:

Calories: 180
Fat: 4.9 gm
Cholesterol: 15 mg
Sodium: 187 mg

Generally, you don't need to sift all–purpose flour before measuring it since it is pre–sifted. On the other hand, cake flour should always be sifted before measuring.

Blue Ribbon Zucchini Bread

*It freezes beautifully. Keep a loaf in the freezer
for spur–of–the–moment entertaining.*

Yield:
2 loaves,
24 slices

Serving Size:
1 slice

Preparation Time:
15–20 minutes

Cooking Time:
45 minutes

**Nutrient Analysis
per serving:**

Calories: 176
Fat: 7 gm
Cholesterol: 34 mg
Sodium: 193 mg

3 eggs, beaten
$\frac{1}{2}$ c. sugar
1 c. brown sugar, packed
$\frac{1}{2}$ c. oil
1 T. maple flavoring
2 c. zucchini, shredded
2 tsp. baking soda
$\frac{1}{2}$ tsp. baking powder
1 tsp. salt
$\frac{1}{2}$ c. wheat germ
2 $\frac{1}{2}$ c. flour
$\frac{1}{3}$ c. walnuts, chopped
Cooking spray
$\frac{1}{4}$ c. sesame seeds

Preheat oven to 350°. Beat together eggs, sugars, oil and maple flavoring until foamy and thick; stir in zucchini. Stir in baking soda, baking powder, salt, wheat germ and flour; mix well. Add nuts. Spoon batter into two 9x5x3-inch loaf pans coated with cooking spray and flour. Sprinkle tops with sesame seeds. Bake 45 minutes to 1 hour, or until toothpick inserted into center comes out clean. Cool 10 minutes before removing from pans.

Resist the temptation to spread margarine or butter on bread. Fresh, flavorful quick breads like Blue Ribbon Zucchini Bread have such a wonderful taste of their own. Why mask it with fatty spreads (not to mention the 36 calories of pure fat in each teaspoonful)!

108

Harvest Pumpkin Bread

When autumn comes, serve this bread warm from the oven with piping hot soup.

2 eggs, beaten

1 c. sugar

1 c. pumpkin, canned

⅓ c. oil

¼ c. water

1 ⅔ c. flour

1 tsp. baking soda

¾ tsp. salt

½ tsp. baking powder

½ tsp. ground cloves

½ tsp. nutmeg

½ tsp. cinnamon

Cooking spray

Yield:
1 loaf
12 slices

Serving Size:
1 slice

Preparation Time:
20 minutes

Cooking Time:
60–70 minutes

Preheat oven to 350°. Combine eggs, sugar, pumpkin, oil and water. Sift flour and remaining ingredients together and add to pumpkin mixture; stir well. Place in an 8½ x 4½ x 2½-inch loaf pan coated with cooking spray and floured. Bake for 60–70 minutes or until loaf sounds hollow when tapped. Allow bread to cool for 10 minutes, then remove from pan.

Nutrient Analysis per serving:

Calories: 195
Fat: 6.9 gm
Cholesterol: 30 mg
Sodium: 253 mg

Place bread in the center of a preheated oven so heat can circulate freely.

Gold Rush Carrot Bread

Truly a 24–karat carrot bread.

Yield:
  1 loaf
  12 slices
Serving Size:
  1 slice
Preparation Time:
  17 minutes
Cooking Time:
  40–50 minutes

**Nutrient Analysis
per serving:**

Calories: 159
Fat: 6.8 gm
Cholesterol: 23 mg
Sodium: 149 mg

½ c. orange juice
⅓ c. oil
¼ c. sugar
1 egg, beaten
2 tsp. vanilla
1 c. whole wheat flour
1 c. flour
1 T. cinnamon
1 tsp. baking powder
½ tsp. baking soda
¼ tsp. salt
1 ¼ c. carrots, grated
Cooking spray

Preheat oven to 350°. Combine orange juice, oil, sugar, egg and vanilla in a large mixing bowl; set aside. Combine whole wheat flour, flour, cinnamon, baking powder, baking soda and salt; mix well. Add dry ingredients to orange juice mixture, stirring just until dry ingredients are moistened. Fold in carrots. Bake in a 9x5x3-inch loaf pan coated with cooking spray for 40–45 minutes or until a wooden pick inserted in center comes out clean.

Baked products that use a combination of all–purpose flour and whole wheat flour have a lighter texture than those that use only whole wheat flour, but more fiber than recipes using only all–purpose flour.

Dude Ranch
Whole Wheat Biscuits

2 c. flour
¾ c. whole wheat flour
4 tsp. baking powder
½ tsp. salt
¼ c. margarine, softened
1 c. skim milk
Cooking spray

Preheat oven to 450°. Combine first 4 ingredients; cut in margarine with a pastry blender until mixture resembles coarse meal. Add milk, stirring until dry ingredients are moistened. Turn dough onto a lightly floured surface; knead about 1 minute. Shape dough into 16 balls and place in a 9-inch square baking pan sprayed with cooking spray. Flatten dough balls slightly; bake 10–12 minutes or until lightly browned.

Yield:
16 biscuits
Serving Size:
1 biscuit
Preparation Time:
15 minutes
Cooking Time:
10–12 minutes

Nutrient Analysis per serving:

Calories: 104
Fat: 3.1 gm
Cholesterol: 0 mg
Sodium: 283 mg

Substituting reduced–calorie margarine for regular margarine works well in many recipes — except baked items. Because reduced–calorie margarines have water whipped into them, the result can be wetter and less flaky baked goods.

Swedish Rye Bread

Yield:
2 loaves
24 slices

Serving Size:
1 slice

Preparation Time:
30 minutes

Rising Time:
75 minutes

Cooking Time:
30–40 minutes

Nutrient Analysis per serving:

Calories: 152
Fat: 1 gm
Cholesterol: 0 mg
Sodium: 279 mg

$^1/_4$ c. warm water (105–115°)
1 pkg. rapid–rise yeast
1 $^1/_2$ c. rye flour
$^1/_4$ c. molasses
$^1/_4$ c. brown sugar, packed
1 T. salt
1 T. caraway seeds
1 T. oil
2 c. warm water (125°)
5 $^1/_2$ c. flour
Cooking spray

Soften yeast in $^1/_4$–$^1/_2$ cup water; let stand 5 minutes. Combine rye flour, molasses, brown sugar, salt, caraway seeds and oil; pour hot water over and mix well. Add yeast and 3 cups white flour; stir well. Continue to add white flour until a soft dough forms. Turn dough out onto a floured surface and knead 10 minutes. Cover and let rise about 1 hour until doubled in bulk. Punch dough down and divide in half. Shape into loaves and put into two 9x5x2-inch loaf pans coated with cooking spray. Let rise again to no more than double in bulk. Bake in a 350° oven for about 30–40 minutes or until loaf sounds hollow when tapped (should be golden brown).

All whole–wheat bread is brown __but__ not all brown bread is whole–wheat. Raisin juice is often added to bread to give it a dark color and create the illusion that it is a whole–wheat product.

Quick Yeast Rolls

Rapid–rise yeast makes this recipe a snap!

3 ½–4 c. flour, divided
1 pkg. rapid–rise yeast
¼ c. sugar
1 tsp. salt
1 c. water
1 ½ T. oil
1 egg
Cooking spray

Set aside one cup of flour for later use. In a large bowl combine remaining flour, yeast, sugar and salt. In microwave, heat water and oil until hot to touch (105–115°). Stir hot liquids into dry mixture. Mix in egg. Mix/knead in enough reserved flour until dough is no longer sticky. Cover dough and let rest for 10 minutes. Shape dough into 16 rolls and place them in two 9-inch round pans that have been coated with cooking spray. Let rise until doubled in size (about 30 minutes). Bake at 350° for 20-25 minutes or until golden brown.

Yield:
16 rolls
Serving Size:
1 roll
Preparation Time:
30 minutes
Rising Time:
30 minutes
Cooking Time:
20–30 minutes

Nutrient Analysis per serving:

Calories: 125
Fat: 1.8 gm
Cholesterol: 11 mg
Sodium: 152 mg

Breads made with quick–rising yeast rise in a third less time than traditional yeast breads. Quick–rising yeast can replace active dry yeast in all recipes except Danish pastry, croissants and those made with a sour-dough starter.

Honey Whole Wheat Bread

Heavy, good–flavored bread — delicious for toast or sandwiches.

Yield:
- 2 loaves
- 40 slices

Serving Size:
- 1 slice

Preparation Time:
- 20 minutes

Rising Time:
- 100 minutes

Cooking Time:
- 55 minutes

Nutrient Analysis per serving:

Calories:	106
Fat:	1.5 gm
Cholesterol:	0 mg
Sodium:	73 mg

1 qt. warm skim milk (105–115°)
2 pkg. rapid–rise yeast
3 T. honey
3 T. oil
1 tsp. salt
8–8 ½ c. whole wheat flour
Cooking spray

Soften yeast in warm milk in a large mixing bowl; let stand 5 minutes. Add honey, oil and salt. Gradually add flour, 1 cup at a time, to make a soft dough. Cover and let rise in a warm place for 1 hour or until doubled in bulk. Turn dough out onto a floured surface and knead until smooth and elastic (about 10 minutes). Divide dough in half and place in two 9x5x3-inch loaf pans coated with cooking spray. Cover and let rise in a warm place for 30 minutes. Bake at 350° for 40–45 minutes or until loaf sounds hollow when tapped.

By law, bread that is labeled "whole wheat" must be made from 100% whole wheat flour. "Stone ground wheat bread," "cracked wheat bread," and "wheat bread" do not contain the term "whole" in their title, and may be made from varying portions of enriched white flour and whole wheat flour.

114

Dilly Casserole Bread

Delicious served warm with Winter Stew.

1 pkg. rapid–rise yeast
1/4 c. warm water (105–115°)
1 c. 1% cottage cheese
2 T. sugar
1 T. margarine, melted
1 T. dried onion flakes
2 tsp. dillseeds
1 tsp. salt
1/4 tsp. baking soda
1 egg, beaten
2 1/2 c. flour
Cooking spray

Soften yeast in warm water in a large mixing bowl; let stand 5 minutes. Combine cottage cheese, sugar, margarine, onion flakes, dillseeds, salt, baking soda and egg; stir until blended. Stir yeast into cottage cheese mixture; gradually stir in flour to make a soft dough. Cover and let rise in a warm place for 50 minutes, or until doubled in bulk. Punch dough down and place in a 2–quart round casserole coated with cooking spray. Cover and let rise in a warm place 40 minutes. Bake at 350° for 40–50 minutes or until golden brown.

Yield:
  1 loaf
  12 slices

Serving Size:
  1 slice

Preparation Time:
  5–10 minutes

Rising Time:
  90 minutes

Cooking Time:
  40–50 minutes

Nutrient Analysis per serving:

Calories: 132
Fat: 1.8 gm
Cholesterol: 16 mg
Sodium: 308 mg

The microwave oven makes a great "warm place" for rising yeast bread. Heat one cup of water for two minutes on full power in microwave. Remove water and place covered dough inside oven to rise.

Make–Ahead Batter
for Bran Muffins

Fresh muffins every morning with ease.

Yield:
  5 dozen
  60 servings

Serving Size:
  1 muffin

Preparation Time:
  15–20 minutes

Cooking Time:
  20 minutes

2 c. boiling water
2 c. shreds of whole bran cereal
5 c. flour
5 tsp. baking soda
2 tsp. salt
2 c. sugar
1 c. margarine, softened
1 c. egg substitute
1 qt. low–fat buttermilk
4 c. whole bran cereal buds
Cooking spray

**Nutrient Analysis
per serving:**

Calories: 119
Fat: 3.7 gm
Cholesterol: 1 mg
Sodium: 256 mg

Preheat oven to 400°. Pour boiling water over shreds of whole bran cereal; set aside. Sift together flour, baking soda and salt. Cream together sugar and margarine in a large mixing bowl until light and fluffy. Add egg substitute and beat well. Blend in buttermilk, bran cereal buds and the soaked whole bran cereal. Stir in dry ingredients until moistened. Store in a tightly covered container in refrigerator. Batter will keep for up to 6 weeks.

To make muffins, fill standard size muffin pan cups coated with cooking spray to ²/₃ full with batter (don't stir batter). Bake for 20 minutes or until done.

Egg substitutes are pasteurized so there is no danger of them containing salmonella. In order to keep this recipe for Make–Ahead Batter for Bran Muffins as safe as possible and cholesterol to a minimum, we chose to use a pasteurized product.

Oatmeal Blueberry Muffins

1 c. flour
1 ½ c. quick–cooking oats, uncooked
1 tsp. cinnamon
1 tsp. baking powder
½ tsp. baking soda
¼ tsp. salt
1 c. low–fat buttermilk
½ c. brown sugar, packed
¼ c. oil
1 egg, beaten
1 c. frozen blueberries
2 T. brown sugar

Yield:
1 ½ dozen
18 servings

Serving Size:
1 muffin

Preparation Time:
10–15 minutes

Cooking Time:
20–25 minutes

Preheat oven to 425°.Combine flour, oats, cinnamon, baking powder, baking soda and salt; set aside. Combine buttermilk, ½ cup brown sugar, oil and egg in a medium mixing bowl; add to flour mixture, mixing just until moist. Fold in blueberries. Fill paper–lined muffin cups to ⅔ full with batter; sprinkle with remaining 2 tablespoons brown sugar. Bake 20–25 minutes or until done.

Nutrient Analysis per serving:

Calories: 119
Fat: 3.9 gm
Cholesterol: 10 mg
Sodium: 112 mg

If you don't have buttermilk on hand when you need it for baking, use this easy substitute: for each cup of buttermilk, place one tablespoon of lemon juice or vinegar in a glass measuring cup and add enough cold milk to make one cup; stir and let stand five minutes before using.

Trail Ride Zucchini Muffins

A great breakfast muffin for the trail.

Yield:
1 ½ dozen
18 servings

Serving Size:
1 muffin

Preparation Time:
15 minutes

Cooking Time:
20 minutes

Nutrient Analysis per serving:

Calories: 154
Fat: 5.6 gm
Cholesterol: 10 mg
Sodium: 115 mg

1 c. whole wheat flour
1 c. flour
2 tsp. baking soda
¼ tsp. baking powder
1 T. cinnamon
1 egg, beaten
⅓ c. oil
¾ c. sugar
½ c. nonfat dry milk
2 ½ c. zucchini, grated
2 tsp. vanilla
1 tsp. lemon extract
½ c. raisins
¼ c. chopped nuts
Cooking spray

Preheat oven to 350°. Sift flours, soda, baking powder and cinnamon together in a bowl; set aside. Combine egg, oil, sugar, dry milk, zucchini, vanilla and lemon extract in another bowl; beat thoroughly. Stir flour mixture into egg mixture just until smooth. Stir in raisins and nuts. Fill standard size muffin cups coated with cooking spray to ⅔ full with batter. Bake for 20 minutes or until done.

Leftover bran muffins make an excellent breakfast sundae. Crumble them in a bowl and top with lowfat yogurt and fresh fruit.

Honey–Lemon Muffins

2 c. flour
2 ½ tsp. baking powder
½ tsp. baking soda
½ tsp. salt
1 T. grated lemon peel
1 egg
¼ c. oil
⅓ c. honey
1 c. plain nonfat yogurt
2 T. lemon juice
Cooking spray

Yield:
  1 dozen
Serving Size:
  1 muffin
Preparation Time:
  20 minutes
Cooking Time:
  18 minutes

Nutrient Analysis per serving:

Calories: 153
Fat: 5.1 gm
Cholesterol: 15 mg
Sodium: 287 mg

Preheat oven to 400°. Combine flour, baking powder, baking soda, salt and grated lemon peel; set aside. Mix egg, oil, honey, yogurt and lemon juice; add to dry ingredients; stirring just until moistened. Fill standard size muffin cups coated with cooking spray ⅔ full with batter. Bake for 18 minutes or until golden brown.

119

Mountain Biker's Banana Muffins

Put these in your pack for a snack while biking.

Yield:
1 dozen

Serving Size:
1 muffin

Preparation Time:
15–20 minutes

Cooking Time:
15–20 minutes

Nutrient Analysis per serving:

Calories: 179
Fat: 6.4 gm
Cholesterol: 0 mg
Sodium: 121 mg

½ c. sugar
1 tsp. baking soda
¼ tsp. salt
¾ c. flour
¾ c. whole wheat flour
⅓ c. oil
¼ c. skim milk
2 large bananas, mashed
1 tsp. vanilla
⅓ c. raisins
Cooking spray

Preheat oven to 375°. Measure sugar, baking soda, salt and flour into bowl. Add oil, milk, bananas and vanilla; mix just until flour is moistened. Fold in raisins. Fill standard size muffin cups coated with cooking spray to ⅔ full with batter. Bake 15–20 minutes or until golden brown. Immediately remove from pan.

Fresh Raspberry Muffins

Mouthwatering, delicious and unbelievably yummy!

1 ¼ c. fresh raspberries

1 ½ c. flour, divided

⅓ c. brown sugar, packed

2 tsp. baking powder

1 tsp. cinnamon

¼ tsp. salt

1 egg, beaten

¼ c. oil

½ c. skim milk

Cooking spray

TOPPING:

3 T. nuts, chopped

2 T. brown sugar

1 tsp. cinnamon

⅓ c. powdered sugar

2 tsp. lemon juice

Yield:
1 dozen
12 servings

Serving Size:
1 muffin

Preparation Time:
25 minutes

Cooking Time:
25 minutes

Nutrient Analysis per serving:

Calories: 165
Fat: 6.3 gm
Cholesterol: 15 mg
Sodium: 60 mg

Preheat oven to 350°. Dust raspberries with 2 tablespoons of flour; set aside. Combine remaining flour, sugar, baking powder, 1 tsp. cinnamon and salt. Combine egg, oil and milk. Add flour mixture to egg mixture alternately with milk. Fold in raspberries. Fill standard size muffin cups coated with cooking spray to ⅔ full with batter. Combine nuts, brown sugar and 1 tsp. cinnamon; sprinkle over muffins and bake 20–25 minutes. Stir together powdered sugar and lemon juice. When muffins are slightly cooled, drizzle sugar/lemon mixture over muffins.

If you want to cut back on the amount of sugar in a recipe, try using brown sugar in place of granulated (white) sugar. Brown sugar's intense flavor allows you to use less than you would with white sugar.

Poppy Seed Poundcake Muffins

Yield:
1 dozen
12 servings

Serving Size:
1 muffin

Preparation Time:
15 minutes

Cooking Time:
20 minutes

¹/₃ c. margarine, softened
³/₄ c. sugar
2 eggs, beaten
2 c. flour
1 T. poppy seeds
¹/₂ tsp. salt
¹/₄ tsp. baking soda
1 c. vanilla low–fat yogurt
1 tsp. vanilla
Cooking spray

*Nutrient Analysis
per serving:*

Calories: 195
Fat: 6.4 gm
Cholesterol: 31 mg
Sodium: 193 mg

Preheat oven to 400°. In a large mixing bowl, cream margarine and sugar with an electric mixer. Add eggs, one at a time, beating after each addition. Combine flour, poppy seeds, salt and baking soda; add to creamed mixture alternately with yogurt, beginning and ending with flour mixture. Mix just until blended after each addition. Stir in vanilla. Fill standard size muffin cups coated with cooking spray to ²/₃ full with batter. Bake 15–20 minutes or until done.

Choose store–bought muffins carefully. Depending on the size, some muffins can have as much fat and calories as doughnuts.

122

PASTA & GRAINS

PASTA & GRAINS

Pasta with Fresh Tomato Sauce

A side dish inspired by Italian tradition. Serve with grilled tuna and a green salad.

3 large tomatoes, cut into ¹/₂-inch pieces
1 clove garlic, minced
1 small onion, finely chopped
1 tsp. dried whole basil
¹/₂ tsp. dried whole oregano
¹/₂ tsp. dried whole rosemary
¹/₂ tsp. salt
Freshly ground black pepper
3 T. olive oil
Juice from 1 lemon
Pinch of cayenne pepper
8 oz. eggless spaghetti, uncooked

Place tomatoes in a bowl with all other ingredients (except pasta); mix well. Cook pasta and toss in bowl with sauce. Serve immediately.

Hint: This pasta dish has a moderate temperature. If you prefer a warm sidedish, heat pasta mixture in the microwave on HIGH for 1–2 minutes.

Yield:
   4 servings
Serving Size:
   1 ¹/₂ cups
Preparation Time:
   10 minutes
Cooking Time:
   12 minutes

Nutrient Analysis per serving:

Calories: 343
Fat: 11.3 gm
Cholesterol: 0 mg
Sodium: 309 mg

The secret to having flavorful tomatoes year 'round is keeping them at room temperature. Refrigerating tomatoes stops the ripening process and kills the tomato flavor. Once ripened, they'll keep a few more days without refrigeration.

Leadville Lasagna

A yummy diversion from traditional lasagna — and easier to make.

Yield:
9 servings

Serving Size:
4x3-inch piece

Preparation Time:
30 minutes

Cooking Time:
30–35 minutes

Nutrient Analysis per serving:

Calories: 321
Fat: 8.1 gm
Cholesterol: 68 mg
Sodium: 551 mg

1 lb. ground turkey

1 c. onion, chopped

2 garlic cloves, minced

1 can (16 oz.) tomatoes, diced

2 cans (8 oz. each) tomato sauce

2 tsp. dried whole basil

1 tsp. dried whole oregano

1 tsp. fennel seed

1 egg

2 c. 1% cottage cheese

$\frac{1}{2}$ c. Parmesan cheese, grated and divided

1 T. dried parsley flakes

$\frac{1}{2}$ tsp. pepper

8 oz. lasagna noodles

8 oz. part–skim mozzarella cheese, shredded

Preheat oven to 375°. In a large nonstick skillet, brown turkey, onion and garlic. Drain off fat. Stir in the next 5 ingredients. Cover and let simmer for 15 minutes, stirring often. Meanwhile, beat egg and combine it with cottage cheese, $\frac{1}{4}$ cup of the Parmesan cheese, parsley and pepper. In the bottom of a 13x9x2-inch baking dish spread $\frac{1}{3}$ of the meat sauce. Rinse noodles with hot water and layer half of them over meat sauce. Spread half of cottage cheese filling over pasta; sprinkle with half the mozzarella cheese. Repeat layers ending with remaining meat sauce. Sprinkle remaining $\frac{1}{4}$ cup Parmesan cheese on top. Bake for 30–35 minutes until heated through.

A time-saving idea used in Leadville Lasagna is to rinse noodles with hot water instead of boiling them. Extra moisture from the sauce is absorbed into the noodles during baking.

126

Red Beans and Rice

½ c. dried red kidney beans

2 c. water

½ c. onion, chopped

¼ c. green bell pepper, chopped

¼ c. green onion, sliced

1 bay leaf

¼ tsp. dried whole thyme

1 clove garlic, minced

⅛ tsp. freshly ground pepper

3 oz. turkey ham, cut into ½-inch cubes
   (optional)

1 c. hot cooked rice, no salt or fat added

Yield:
   2 servings
Serving Size:
   1 ½ cups
Preparation Time:
   20 minutes
Cooking Time:
   1-1/2 hours

*Nutrient Analysis
per serving:*

Calories: 275
Fat: .8 gm
Cholesterol: 0 mg
Sodium: 15 mg

Put all ingredients except rice in a saucepan and simmer covered for 1 ½ hours, or until beans are tender and sauce is thick. Spoon ½ cup of rice onto each plate and ladle the red bean mixture over or around the rice.

Note: You may want to add the turkey ham during the last 30 minutes of cooking so it does not become too tender and fall apart. For fairly firm beans and a thick gravy, mash ½ cup of the cooked beans and stir them back into the pot.

Crowd out fatty foods in your diet by filling up on complex carbo-hydrates: legumes, grains, pastas, breads, cereals and vegetables.

Dove Creek Anasazi Beans

Locally–produced Anasazi beans are a naturally sweet alternative to regular baked beans.

Yield:
6 cups
12 servings

Serving Size:
$^1/_2$ cup

Preparation Time:
10 minutes

Cooking Time:
1–1 $^1/_4$ hours

Nutrient Analysis per serving:

Calories: 153
Fat: 1.1 gm
Cholesterol: 5 mg
Sodium: 324 mg

1 pkg. (16 oz.) dried Anasazi beans or pinto beans
6 c. water
$^3/_4$ c. (4 oz.) lean cooked ham, chopped
$^3/_4$ c. onion, chopped
2 cloves garlic, minced
1 $^1/_2$ T. chili powder
$^1/_2$ tsp. pepper
$^1/_2$ tsp. salt
1 can (10 oz.) diced tomatoes and green chilies, undrained

Sort and wash beans; place in a Dutch oven. Cover with water 2 inches above beans; let soak 8 hours. Drain beans and return to Dutch oven. Add 6 cups water and next 6 ingredients. Bring to a boil; reduce heat and simmer 45 minutes (or until beans are tender), stirring occasionally. Add tomatoes and simmer 15 minutes longer.

Anasazi beans have a sweeter flavor and cook faster than most beans. They were one of the crops that was originally cultivated by the Anasazi Indians.

128

Tabor Tabbouleh

Be adventurous — try it!

1 c. bulgur or cracked wheat
2 medium tomatoes
1 medium cucumber, peeled
5 green onions
³/₄ c. fresh parsley, chopped
1 T. mint, chopped
1 T. oil
¹/₄ tsp. dried whole oregano
¹/₄ tsp. cumin
Juice from 1 lemon
Salt and pepper to taste

Wash cracked wheat in cold water; drain. Chop tomatoes, cucumber, onions, parsley and mint very fine. Add oregano and cumin to chopped ingredients; combine with wheat. Add oil, seasonings and lemon juice. Refrigerate until wheat softens. Serve.

Yield:
  6 servings
Serving Size:
  ¹/₂ cup
Preparation Time:
  15 minutes

Nutrient Analysis per serving:

Calories: 150
Fat: 2.9 gm
Cholesterol: 0 mg
Sodium: 109 mg

Whole grains are products that contain the entire grain. They include the bran and germ portions that contain most of the fiber. Remember, whole grain doesn't have to mean bread or cereal — try bulgur, corn tortillas, brown rice and popcorn to increase the fiber in your diet.

Sweet & Sour Lentils

An excellent meatless meal served with whole–wheat bread and vegetable sticks.

Yield:
6 servings

Serving Size:
$\frac{1}{2}$ cup

Preparation Time:
5 minutes

Cooking Time:
25–30 minutes

Nutrient Analysis per serving:

Calories: 183
Fat: 5.6 gm
Cholesterol: 0 mg
Sodium: 139 mg

2 $\frac{1}{2}$ c. chicken broth
1 c. red or green lentils
$\frac{1}{2}$ c. onion, chopped
2 T. oil
4–6 T. lemon juice
1 $\frac{1}{2}$ to 2 T. sugar
Salt and pepper to taste
2 T. fresh parsley or cilantro, minced
Paprika
Lettuce leaves

Heat broth and lentils in 2–quart saucepan; bring to a boil. Reduce heat and simmer 20–30 minutes until lentils are done but haven't lost shape. Stir in remaining ingredients, first adding lesser amounts of lemon juice and sugar and increasing amount for desired flavor. Stir carefully. Sprinkle with paprika. Serve warm or cold on a bed of lettuce leaves.

Mexican Bulgur

A nice mix of bulgur wheat and the Mexican spices that Coloradans love.

1 T. margarine
1 medium onion, finely chopped
1 green pepper, finely chopped
1 c. bulgur or cracked wheat
2 c. chicken broth
1 tsp. chili powder
½ tsp. ground cumin
Salsa

Yield:
6 servings

Serving Size:
²/₃ cup

Preparation Time:
12 minutes

Cooking Time:
25 minutes

In a large skillet, heat margarine Add onion and green pepper; saute' over medium heat for 6–7 minutes (or until soft), stirring occasionally. Add bulgur and cook 2 minutes, stirring to coat the grains. Add remaining ingredients and bring to a boil. Cover, reduce heat and simmer slowly for 15 minutes or until liquid has absorbed. Serve hot, garnished with salsa.

Nutrient Analysis per serving:

Calories: 150
Fat: 3.1 gm
Cholesterol: 0 mg
Sodium: 58 mg

Garden Rice

Yield:
6 servings

Serving Size:
$\frac{1}{2}$ cup

Preparation Time:
10 minutes

Cooking Time:
40 minutes

Nutrient Analysis per serving:

Calories: 142
Fat: .7 gm
Cholesterol: 0 mg
Sodium: 210 mg

1 c. brown rice
2 cloves garlic, minced
$\frac{1}{2}$ tsp. salt
$\frac{1}{2}$ tsp. paprika
$\frac{1}{8}$ tsp. cayenne pepper
$\frac{1}{2}$ lb. fresh green beans, cut into 1-inch pieces
1 c. small cauliflower flowerets
$\frac{1}{4}$ c. plain nonfat yogurt, room temperature

Cook rice according to package directions with garlic, salt, paprika and cayenne pepper. Meanwhile, steam beans and cauliflower until tender (about 6 minutes); set aside. Add steamed vegetables to rice during the last 5 minutes of cooking. Just before serving, stir in yogurt.

Brown rice has a brown color because it contains the tough, darker layer of the rice kernel. That extra layer is also called the bran, and it is rich in vitamin E, phosphorus, riboflavin and calcium.

Berthoud Pass Bulgur

Serve this whole–grain dish with our Chicken in Orange–Almond Sauce — then wait for the raves.

2 T. margarine
½ c. celery, chopped
1 medium onion, chopped
1 c. fresh mushrooms, sliced
1 c. bulgur or cracked wheat
¼ tsp. dried dillweed
¼ tsp. dried whole oregano
½ tsp. salt (optional)
¼ tsp. pepper
2 c. low–sodium chicken broth

Melt margarine in a large skillet; add celery, onion and mushrooms. Stir constantly until vegetables are tender. Add bulgur and cook until golden. Add seasonings and chicken broth; cover and bring to a boil. Reduce heat and simmer 15 minutes. Serve hot.

Yield:
8 servings
Serving Size:
½ cup
Preparation Time:
10 minutes
Cooking Time:
30 minutes

Nutrient Analysis per serving:

Calories: 123
Fat: 3.7 gm
Cholesterol: 0 mg
Sodium: 61 mg

Bulgur consists of wheat kernels that have been steamed, dried and crushed. It is often confused with, but is not exactly the same as, cracked wheat — which is the whole unprocessed wheat kernel broken into fragments. They can be used interchangeably in most recipes.

Savory Green Rice

Yield:
   8 servings

Serving Size:
   $1/2$ cup

Preparation Time:
   10 minutes

Cooking Time:
   10 minutes

*Nutrient Analysis
per serving:*

Calories: 85
Fat: .4 gm
Cholesterol: 0 mg
Sodium: 41 mg

1 $1/2$ c. low–sodium chicken broth
$1/3$ c. green onions, sliced
2 cloves garlic, minced
$1/2$ tsp. dried whole basil
$1/2$ tsp. pepper
$1/2$ tsp. dried whole thyme
1 pkg. (10 oz.) frozen chopped spinach,
   thawed and drained
1 $1/2$ c. instant rice

In a large microwave–safe bowl, combine chicken broth, onion, garlic and seasonings. Microwave on HIGH for 3 minutes. Add spinach and continue to cook on high until mixture comes to a boil. Remove from microwave and stir in rice. Cover and let stand for 5 minutes. Serve as an accompaniment to your favorite poultry or fish entree.

Spicy Fruited Rice

*This jazzed–up rice goes well
with roasted fowl.*

1 c. rice, uncooked

$1/2$ c. raisins

$1/2$ c. celery, chopped

$1/2$ c. onion, chopped

1 T. margarine

$1/2$ tsp. cinnamon

$1/4$ tsp. allspice

$1/8$ tsp. pepper

1 tart apple, chopped

$1/4$ c. sliced almonds, toasted

Yield:
  6 servings

Serving Size:
  $2/3$ cup

Preparation Time:
  15 minutes

Cooking Time:
  20 minutes

**Nutrient Analysis
per serving:**

Calories: 169
Fat: 5.2 gm
Cholesterol: 0 mg
Sodium: 34 mg

Cook rice according to package directions, stirring raisins into rice for the last 5 minutes of cooking time. In a large nonstick skillet, saute' celery and onion in margarine until vegetables are tender, yet crisp. Stir in seasonings and rice; heat thoroughly. Add apple; cover and let stand 5 minutes. Sprinkle with almonds and serve.

Alpine Rice and Mushrooms

Yield:
8 servings

Serving Size:
½ cup

Preparation Time:
8 minutes

Cooking Time:
50 minutes

**Nutrient Analysis
per serving:**

Calories: 115
Fat: 2 gm
Cholesterol: 0 mg
Sodium: 95 mg

1 c. brown rice, uncooked
2 c. mushrooms, sliced
⅓ c. green onions, sliced
1 T. margarine
¼ c. fresh parsley, chopped
¼ c. dry white wine
1 T. lemon juice
¼ tsp. salt

Cook rice according to package directions. In a medium nonstick skillet saute' mushrooms and green onions in margarine. Add parsley, wine, lemon juice and salt; remove from heat. Stir hot rice into mushroom mixture and serve.

Mushrooms are an excellent addition to favorite recipes. They provide bulk and texture, but contribute only 18 calories per cup and no fat.

FISH & SEAFOOD

FISH & SEAFOOD

Garlic Shrimp on a Bun

Great for a light lunch on the deck.

Cooking spray
¼ c. green onion, sliced
2–3 cloves garlic, minced
2 tsp. olive oil
⅔ c. white wine
¼ c. lemon juice
⅛ tsp. salt
⅛ tsp. pepper
1 tsp. dried dillweed
1 ½ lbs. medium–size raw shrimp,
peeled and deveined
3 French rolls, split lengthwise and toasted

In a nonstick skillet coated with cooking spray, sauté onion and garlic until tender; add wine, lemon juice, salt, pepper and dillweed. Bring mixture to a boil and let simmer 5 minutes to blend flavors. Add shrimp and cook 3–5 minutes longer until shrimp are opaque. Spoon over toasted rolls and serve immediately.

Yield:
6 servings

Serving Size:
½ roll with
4 oz. shrimp

Preparation Time:
5–10 minutes

Cooking Time:
15 minutes

Nutrient Analysis per serving:

Calories: 183
Fat: 3.1 gm
Cholesterol: 125 mg
Sodium: 360 mg

Always purchase seafood and shellfish at reputable stores to ensure its quality and safety. Purchasing fish at roadside sales may be tempting, but your health could be at stake if the fish was harvested from unsafe waters.

Italian Fish in Foil

*A great make–ahead meal for company.
Simply remove the prepared foil packets
from your refrigerator and slip them on the grill.*

Yield:
4 servings

Serving Size:
6-ounce portion

Preparation Time:
15–20 minutes

Cooking Time:
20 minutes

**Nutrient Analysis
per serving:**

Calories: 220
Fat: 1.5 gm
Cholesterol: 121 mg
Sodium: 535 mg

Cooking spray
2 T. green onions, sliced
¾ c. dry white wine
½ c. fresh mushrooms, sliced
1 T. cornstarch
⅓ c. water
**1 can (16 oz.) Italian–style tomatoes with
  basil, drained**
2 T. lemon juice
2 T. parsley, minced
½ tsp. pepper
¼ tsp. salt
1 lb. sole (or cod) fillets
**1 c. fresh or frozen raw shrimp, peeled
  and deveined**

Coat a medium nonstick skillet with cooking spray. Add onions and sauté over medium heat until tender; stir in wine and mushrooms and continue to cook until mushrooms are tender. Mix cornstarch with ⅓ cup water until smooth; stir into mushroom mix. Cook, stirring constantly, until mixture boils and thickens. Continue to cook and stir for 1 minute; stir in tomatoes, lemon juice, parsley, pepper and salt. Place equal portions of fish on each of 4 pieces of heavy–duty aluminum foil. Divide the shrimp and tomato sauce mixture equally among the portions of fish. Seal fish in foil and place on grill 4–6 inches from medium–hot coals. Cook for 15 minutes on grill or bake in 400° oven for about 15–20 minutes or until fish flakes easily when tested with a fork.

Shrimp Jambalaya

2 c. cooked rice
1 medium onion, chopped
$1/2$ green pepper, chopped
$1/2$ c. mushrooms, chopped
2 tsp. oil
2 cans ($14^1/2$ oz. each) Cajun–style tomatoes
1 T. flour
$1/2$ tsp. garlic powder
$1/2$ tsp. dried whole thyme
$1/8$ tsp. cayenne pepper
$1/8$ tsp. ground cloves
2 bay leaves
1 c. cooked ham, chopped
1 pkg. (6 oz.) frozen cooked shrimp

Cook rice according to package directions; set aside. In a Dutch oven, sauté onion, green pepper and mushrooms in oil. Add tomatoes and stir. Sprinkle mixture with flour; cook and stir for 4 minutes. Stir in the next 5 ingredients; cook for 4 minutes. Reduce to simmer. Stir in ham, shrimp and cooked rice. Simmer for 20 minutes. Stir occasionally and add water if necessary.

Yield:
6 servings
Serving Size:
1 cup
Preparation Time:
10–15 minutes
Cooking Time:
35–40 minutes

Nutrient Analysis per serving:

Calories:	205
Fat:	3.5 gm
Cholesterol:	67 mg
Sodium:	697 mg

Fresh fish is best when it's cooked and eaten the same day it's purchased. When that isn't possible, store fish on ice in the coldest part of the refrigerator.

Spicy Shrimp Boil

A unique shrimp dish cooked in a spicy broth.

Yield:
  4 servings

Serving Size:
  1 ½ cups

Preparation Time:
  5 minutes

Standing Time:
  1–2 hours

Cooking Time:
  40–50 minutes

½ c. lemon juice
¼ c. olive oil
¼ c. brown sugar, packed
1 ½ T. Worcestershire sauce
2 tsp. Italian seasoning
2 cloves garlic, minced
1 tsp. pepper
¼–½ tsp. crushed red pepper flakes
1 tsp. dried whole rosemary
1 c. brown rice
1 lb. raw shrimp, peeled and deveined

Nutrient Analysis per serving:

Calories: 453
Fat: 15.7 gm
Cholesterol: 165 mg
Sodium: 261 mg

In large saucepan, mix all ingredients except rice and shrimp. Let mixture stand 1–2 hours before cooking to blend flavors. Meanwhile, cook rice according to package directions. Ten minutes before serving time, bring spice mixture to a boil; add shrimp and cook until shrimp are opaque. Serve over rice.

New analyses demonstrate that cholesterol values for shellfish are far lower than previously thought. Shrimp, clams, scallops and lobster are now considered good selections, particularly since they are naturally low in calories and fat.

142

Backyard Grilled Tuna Steaks

4 (5 oz. each) tuna steaks
½ c. oil–free Italian dressing
2 tsp. low–sodium soy sauce
2 tsp. lemon juice

Place tuna steaks in a 2-inch deep dish. Combine Italian dressing, soy sauce and lemon juice; pour over tuna steaks. Cover and refrigerate 1 hour, turning once. Remove steaks from marinade and reserve marinade. Grill tuna over medium coals for 5 minutes on each side or until fish flakes easily when tested with a fork, basting occasionally with marinade.

Yield:
  4 servings

Serving Size:
  5 ounces

Preparation Time:
  5 minutes

Marinating Time:
  1 hour

Cooking Time:
  10 minutes

Nutrient Analysis
per serving:

Calories: 218
Fat: 6.9 gm
Cholesterol: 53 mg
Sodium: 80 mg

When handling raw poultry, meat or fish, wash your hands, the counters, utensils and cutting boards with hot, soapy water between recipe steps. Never put cooked poultry, meat or fish on the plate that held it when it was uncooked, unless the plate has since been washed.

Teriyaki Swordfish

Teriyaki marinades may be "a dime a dozen," but this one is flavorful <u>without</u> oil.

Yield:
4 servings

Serving Size:
6 ounces

Preparation Time:
5 minutes

Marinating Time:
2 hours

Cooking Time:
15–30 minutes

**Nutrient Analysis
per serving:**

Calories: 207
Fat: 5 gm
Cholesterol: 48 mg
Sodium: 260 mg

1 c. white or rose wine
¼ c. low–sodium soy sauce
2 cloves garlic, minced
2 tsp. ginger
1 tsp. dried whole oregano
Pepper to taste
4 (6 oz. each) swordfish steaks (halibut or
     salmon can be substituted)

Combine first 6 ingredients and pour over swordfish steaks. Cover and marinate several hours or overnight in the refrigerator. Grill swordfish about 10–15 minutes, depending on thickness of steaks, basting occasionally with marinade; OR bake at 350° for 30–35 minutes in marinade. Remove from marinade and serve.

*Fish that is fresh has practically no "fish" odor. The fish odor becomes more pro-nounced with the passage of time, but the odor should **not** be strong when the fish is bought.*

Honey Mustard Salmon

2 T. rum
4 tsp. Dijon mustard
1 T. honey
1 T. lemon juice
¼ tsp. pepper
2 (5 oz. each) salmon steaks

In a small mixing bowl, whisk together the first 5 ingredients. Brush both sides of each salmon steak with marinade. Cover and refrigerate several hours. Grill fish over medium–hot coals, turning once, until steaks flake easily when tested with a fork. OR, broil 6 inches from heat 6–8 minutes longer, or until done.

Yield:
2 servings
Serving Size:
5 ounces
Preparation Time:
5–10 minutes
Marinating Time:
2–4 hours
Cooking Time:
10–15 minutes

Nutrient Analysis
per serving:

Calories: 293
Fat: 9 gm
Cholesterol: 55 mg
Sodium: 205 mg

Questions about fish? Call the American Seafood Institute's toll–free hotline at 1–800–EAT–FISH between 9:00 a.m. and 5:00 p.m., eastern time.

Wine–Baked Salmon with Tarragon Sauce

So elegant they'll think you've been cooking all day. (But we know how truly simple this recipe really is!)

Yield:
4 servings

Serving Size:
6 ounces

Preparation Time:
5 minutes

Cooking Time:
10–15 minutes

Nutrient Analysis per serving:

Calories:	290
Fat:	10.2 gm
Cholesterol:	62 mg
Sodium:	261 mg

4 (6 oz. each) salmon steaks
½ c. dry white wine
1 ½ tsp. dried tarragon, divided
1 c. plain nonfat yogurt
3 T. Dijon mustard
Lemon slices
Fresh parsley

Preheat oven to 350°. Rinse salmon, pat dry. Place salmon in baking dish coated with cooking spray. Pour wine over fish; sprinkle with ½ tsp. dried tarragon. Bake fish for 10–15 minutes or until salmon flakes easily when tested with a fork. Meanwhile, in medium saucepan, slowly warm yogurt, mustard and 1 tsp. tarragon, stirring occasionally. Divide sauce among 4 heated plates. Place salmon on top of sauce and garnish with lemon slices and fresh parsley.

If by mistake a dish made with yogurt boils and curdles, it's still okay to eat — the appearance is just not as pleasing.

146

Linguine with Salmon and Lemon Sauce

For an easy end to a hectic day — keep ingredients for this quick meal in your pantry.

8 oz. spinach linguine

2 T. olive oil

1/2 c. onion, sliced

2 cloves garlic, minced

1/2 tsp. lemon peel, grated

1/3 c. lemon juice

2 T. fresh parsley, chopped

1 can (7-3/4 oz.) salmon, drained, OR leftover salmon

2 T. Parmesan cheese, grated

Cook pasta according to package directions. While pasta is cooking, prepare sauce. Heat oil in a large skillet over low heat; add onion and saute' until tender. Add garlic; saute' another 2 minutes. Stir in lemon peel, lemon juice and parsley. Add salmon and carefully break up meat with a fork. Do not stir. Toss linguine and sauce together. Sprinkle with Parmesan cheese and serve immediately.

Yield:
4 servings

Serving Size:
1 1/4 cups

Preparation Time:
10 minutes

Cooking Time:
15 minutes

Nutrient Analysis per serving:

Calories: 370
Fat: 11.8 gm
Cholesterol: 32 mg
Sodium: 356 mg

Lemon zest, the yellow–colored part of the lemon rind, is often used in recipes since a small quantity of lemon zest can add a much stronger lemon flavor than lemon juice alone.

Cheese–Topped Orange Roughy

An amiable blending of Parmesan cheese and fish — soon to be a favorite.

Yield:
6 servings

Serving Size:
5 ounces

Preparation Time:
3–5 minutes

Cooking Time:
10–12 minutes

Nutrient Analysis per serving:

Calories: 134
Fat: 4.5 gm
Cholesterol: 53 mg
Sodium: 211 mg

Cooking spray

2 lb. orange roughy (sole, cod or snapper can be substituted)

TOPPING:

⅓ c. light mayonnaise

⅓ c. Parmesan cheese, grated

¼ c. green onion, sliced

½ tsp. lemon juice

¼–½ tsp. garlic powder

Hot sauce to taste

Preheat oven to 350°. Place fish in a shallow glass casserole coated with cooking spray; bake 8 minutes or until fish flakes easily when tested with a fork. Meanwhile, mix topping ingredients. Spread topping evenly over cooked fish fillets. Broil 6 inches from heat for 5 minutes or until topping is lightly browned.

Fresh Parmesan cheese has a stronger flavor than the box variety, so less can be used in recipes without sacrificing flavor.

Steamed Halibut with Roasted Red Pepper Sauce

This tremendous sauce is worth the extra effort.

2 large sweet red peppers
1 tsp. olive oil
1/2 c. onion, chopped
2 cloves garlic, minced
1/2 tsp. dried whole oregano
OR 1 1/2 tsp. fresh oregano
1/4–1/2 c. low–sodium chicken broth
1 T. vinegar
4 (6 oz. each) halibut steaks

Broil peppers on top rack of oven, turning every few minutes until evenly cooked (peppers are done when they blister). Place peppers in a small paper bag and let cool 15–20 minutes; remove from bag, peel and seed. Cut peppers into chunks. Heat oil in a nonstick skillet over medium heat. Add onion and garlic; sauté until tender. Place onion mixture, roasted pepper chunks, oregano and vinegar in blender. Add 2 tablespoons broth and process; continue to add broth until desired consistency. Set aside.

Bring about 2 inches of water to boil in a large Dutch oven. Sprinkle halibut steaks with salt and pepper; place steaks in a vegetable steamer and place steamer into Dutch oven. Cover and steam 12–15 minutes or until fish flakes easily when tested with a fork. Serve with red pepper sauce.

Yield:
4 servings

Serving Size:
6 ounces

Preparation Time:
25 minutes

Cooking Time:
15 minutes

Nutrient Analysis per serving:

Calories: 214
Fat: 5.3 gm
Cholesterol: 52 mg
Sodium: 95 mg

Fish marked "fresh" means that it has never been frozen — not that it was caught just hours ago.

Chinese–Style Poached Fish

Yield:
  6 servings

Serving Size:
  1 filet with
  1 T. sauce

Preparation Time:
  10 minutes

Cooking Time:
  10 minutes

3 c. water
6 fish fillets (cod, sole or other white fish)
  (about 6 oz. each)
¹/₂ c. green onion, sliced
¹/₄ c. low–sodium soy sauce
3 T. rice vinegar
1 tsp. sesame oil
3 T. grated fresh gingerroot
2–3 T. water
Pepper to taste

**Nutrient Analysis
per serving:**

Calories: 155
Fat: 1.9 gm
Cholesterol: 70 mg
Sodium: 202 mg

Bring water to boil in a large skillet. Place fish fillets in the boiling water, cover and reduce heat to a simmer. Poach fish about 5–7 minutes, or until fish flakes easily when tested with a fork. While fish is cooking, heat onions, soy sauce, rice vinegar, sesame oil, ginger, water and pepper in a small sauce pan. Remove fish from water with a slotted spoon and transfer to a plate. Spoon ginger sauce over fish and serve immediately.

Bay Scallops with Pepper and Pasta

A beautiful green, red and white presentation in a light sauce

2 c. thin spinach pasta, uncooked
1 T. margarine
1/2 lb. bay scallops
1 large red pepper, cut into strips
1/2 c. dry white wine
1/4 c. lemon juice
1 clove garlic, minced

Cook pasta according to package directions. Melt margarine in a medium nonstick skillet; add scallops and pepper, cook until scallops are opaque. Remove scallop–pepper mixture from pan; set aside. To skillet, add wine, lemon juice and garlic; reduce to about half the original volume. Stir in pasta and scallop–pepper mixture. Heat and serve.

Yield:
4 servings

Serving Size:
1 1/2 cup

Preparation Time:
10 minutes

Cooking Time:
15 minutes

Nutrient Analysis per serving:

Calories: 209
Fat: 4.1 gm
Cholesterol: 22 mg
Sodium: 153 mg

When buying scallops, look for firm, distinctive shapes. Scallops that appear to be melting into one another are past their prime.

Fish Ole '

Fish takes on a new twist when baked with a Mexican flair.

Yield:
4 servings

Serving Size:
5 ounces

Preparation Time:
5 minutes

Cooking Time:
20–25 minutes

Cooking spray

1 ½ lb. white fish (i.e., pollack, snapper, cod fillets)

1 c. prepared salsa

4 oz. reduced–fat Monterey Jack cheese, shredded

Preheat oven to 350°. Wash fish fillets and dry. Place fillets in a 13x9x2-inch glass casserole dish coated with cooking spray; pour salsa over fish. Sprinkle with shredded cheese. Bake 20–25 minutes or until fish flakes easily when tested with a fork.

Nutrient Analysis per serving:

Calories: 234
Fat: 9 gm
Cholesterol: 0 mg
Sodium: 687 mg

Recently, several studies have found that as few as two fish meals per week may reduce the risk of heart disease. The benefits of fish are partially due to Omega-3 fatty acids, a polyunsaturated fat that may make artery walls less prone to blood clot formation.

152

Fettuccine with Shrimp Sauce

8 oz. eggless spinach fettuccine noodles
1 ¹/₂ c. low–sodium chicken broth
¹/₄ c. dry white wine
¹/₄ tsp. dried whole marjoram
Dash of pepper
³/₄ lb. fresh or frozen raw shrimp, peeled
   and deveined
1 T. cornstarch
1 c. skim milk
2 slices (1 oz. each) low–fat processed Swiss
   cheese, cut up
2 T. snipped chives or green onion tops

Yield:
   4 servings
Serving Size:
   1 ¹/₂ cups
Preparation Time:
   15 minutes
Cooking Time:
   30–35 minutes

Nutrient Analysis per serving:

Calories:	369
Fat:	5.7 gm
Cholesterol:	137 mg
Sodium:	426 mg

Cook pasta according to package directions; set aside. Meanwhile, combine chicken broth, wine, marjoram and pepper in a saucepan; bring to a boil. Add shrimp and return mixture to boiling. Cook 1 minute or until shrimp are opaque. Remove shrimp from sauce into another dish; cover and set aside. Bring broth mixture to a full boil; boil 20 minutes or until sauce is reduced to ¹/₂ cup. Combine cornstarch and milk; add to reduced mixture in saucepan. Cook sauce 2 minutes or until thickened and bubbly. Add cheese and chives; stir until cheese is melted. Return shrimp to saucepan; heat through. Serve over pasta.

The best test for seafood freshness is the sniff test — if seafood smells strong, "fishy" or like ammonia, don't buy it.

Fish in Creamy Dill Sauce

Marvelous, and low–calorie too!

Yield:
4 servings

Serving Size:
5 ounces

Preparation Time:
3–5 minutes

Cooking Time:
10 minutes

Nutrient Analysis per serving:

Calories: 130
Fat: 1.3 gm
Cholesterol: 52 mg
Sodium: 208 mg

1 c. plain nonfat yogurt
2 T. Dijon mustard
1 tsp. dried dillweed
1 ½ lb. fish (sole, halibut, swordfish)

Combine yogurt, mustard and dill; set aside for 20 minutes to allow flavors to blend. Steam, broil or grill fish until fish flakes easily when tested with a fork. Spoon *Creamy Dill Sauce* over fish and serve.

The 10–Minute Rule of fish cookery applies anytime you are grilling, broiling, poaching or sautéing fish. Measure the fish at its thickest point, then cook the fish for about 10 minutes per inch of thickness (turning it halfway through the cooking time).

Clam–Filled Lasagna Rolls

8 lasagna noodle strips
1 can (6$\frac{1}{2}$ oz.) chopped clams,
**   reserve liquid**
2 c. commercial low–fat spaghetti sauce
1 container (15 oz.) lite ricotta cheese
$\frac{1}{2}$ c. Parmesan cheese, grated
1 egg, beaten
1 T. dried parsley flakes

Cook noodles according to package directions and drain. Preheat oven to 350°. Combine clam liquid and spaghetti sauce. Spoon half of the sauce into a 9x9-inch baking dish and spread until dish bottom is covered. In a medium bowl, combine clams, ricotta, Parmesan, egg and parsley; mix well. Spread equal portions of clam/cheese mixture on entire length of lasagna noodles and roll up jellyroll fashion. Place, seam side down, in prepared baking dish. Top with remaining sauce; cover. Bake 35–45 minutes or until hot.

Yield:
    4 servings
Serving Size:
    2 rolls
Preparation Time:
    15–20 minutes
Cooking Time:
    35–40 minutes

Nutrient Analysis per serving:

Calories: 435
Fat: 15 gm
Cholesterol: 116 mg
Sodium: 479 mg

Most pasta is made from durum semolina. This type of wheat has a slightly higher protein content than wheat used in bread products.

Landlubber's Salmon Patties

*Including more fish in your diet
was never so easy.*

Yield:
4 servings

Serving Size:
4-ounce patty

Preparation Time:
5 minutes

Cooking Time:
10–15 minutes

**Nutrient Analysis
per serving:**

Calories: 220
Fat: 11 gm
Cholesterol: 106 mg
Sodium: 652 mg

1 can (15.5 oz.) pink salmon, drained
1 whole egg OR 2 egg whites
½ c. crushed cornflake cereal
¼ c. onion, minced
2 T. lemon juice
1 T. oil

Mash salmon with fork. Add egg whites, crushed cereal, onion and lemon juice. Mix thoroughly; form 4 patties. Heat oil over medium heat in a nonstick skillet. Add patties and cook 6–8 minutes or until brown; turn and cook 4–6 minutes or until brown.

Canned fish such as salmon and sardines can be a good source of calcium because the bones are never removed before canning.

Lemon Grilled Trout

When you're lucky enough to have fresh trout, use this grilling idea at home or over a campfire.

4 whole pan–sized trout, cleaned
1 lemon, sliced
2 tsp. oil

Insert several slices of lemon into the cavity of each trout; brush the outside of each fish with oil. Grill over high heat for 5–7 minutes per side, or until fish flakes easily when tested with a fork. Serve whole trout with extra lemon wedges and *Cucumber Dill Sauce* on the side.

Yield:
4 servings

Serving Size:
1 trout

Preparation Time:
5 minutes

Cooking Time:
10–14 minutes

Nutrient Analysis per serving:

Calories: 153
Fat: 6 gm
Cholesterol: 61 mg
Sodium: 29 mg

Cucumber Dill Sauce

1 c. plain nonfat yogurt
¼ c. light mayonnaise
1 c. cucumber, peeled, grated and drained
1 tsp. dried dillweed
½ tsp. lemon juice
½ tsp. pepper

In a blender, combine yogurt and light mayonnaise; process until smooth. Stir in remaining ingredients. Serve as a sauce on baked chicken or fish, or as a vegetable dip.

Yield:
1 ½ cups
6 servings

Serving Size:
¼ cup

Preparation Time:
5 minutes

Nutrient Analysis per serving:

Calories: 37
Fat: 1.9 gm
Cholesterol: 2 mg
Sodium: 73 mg

Trout Almondine

*A special way to prepare your
freshly–caught trout.*

Yield:
  4 servings

Serving Size:
  1 fillet

Preparation Time:
  8 minutes

Cooking Time:
  15–20 minutes

**Nutrient Analysis
per serving:**

Calories: 253
Fat: 8.2 gm
Cholesterol: 62 mg
Sodium: 205 mg

4 trout fillets
¹⁄₄ c. flour
¹⁄₄ c. cornmeal
¹⁄₄ tsp. salt
¹⁄₄ tsp. pepper
¹⁄₂ c. skim milk
Cooking spray
1 tsp. margarine
3 T. slivered almonds
2 T. white wine
4 lemon wedges

Preheat oven to 400°. Combine cornmeal, flour, salt and pepper. Dip fillets in skim milk then dredge in cornmeal mixture. Coat a baking rack (a cake cooling rack works well) with cooking spray; place rack in a jelly roll pan. Place trout fillets on rack and bake for 15–20 minutes or until fish flakes easily when tested with a fork. Meanwhile, sauté almonds in margarine; add wine. Pour evenly over cooked fish. Serve with a lemon wedge.

Oilier cold–water fish such as trout, salmon, mackerel, herring, sardines, fresh tuna and whitefish contain the omega–3 fatty acids that have been shown to help pre-vent heart disease.

POULTRY

Grilled Chicken with White Barbeque Sauce

Served with a colorful mixed green salad, this unique dish is a winner.

¾ c. fat–free mayonnaise
¼ c. cider vinegar
⅛ c. lemon juice
1 T. sugar
1 tsp. white pepper
1 T. white wine Worcestershire sauce
4 boneless chicken breast halves, skinned

Combine first 6 ingredients in a small bowl; mix well. Arrange chicken in a shallow baking dish. Pour 1 cup sauce mixture over chicken, turning to coat. Cover and chill remaining sauce. Cover and chill chicken 6–8 hours, turning occasionally. Remove chicken, reserving marinade. Grill chicken over medium–hot coals 10 minutes or until done, turning once and basting with reserved marinade. Serve chicken with chilled white barbeque sauce.

Yield:
  4 servings

Serving Size:
  1 chicken breast
  half

Preparation Time:
  5 minutes

Marinating Time:
  6–8 hours

Cooking Time:
  10 minutes

Nutrient Analysis per serving:

Calories: 225
Fat: 4 gm
Cholesterol: 96 mg
Sodium: 157 mg

When shopping, you can determine if chicken or beef has been previously frozen by looking at the tray packaging. A large pool of juices around the meat is a result of previous freezing.

Tandoori Chicken

*Served cold, it makes an elegant picnic
for a concert at the Botanic Gardens.*

Yield:
  4 servings

Serving Size:
  1 chicken breast
  half with
  $1/4$ of sauce

Preparation Time:
  10 minutes

Marinating Time:
  2 hours—1day

Cooking Time:
  40–45 minutes

**Nutrient Analysis
per serving:**

Calories: 169
Fat: 3.2 gm
Cholesterol: 72 mg
Sodium: 521 mg

1 c. plain nonfat yogurt
1 T. fresh lemon juice
1 T. low–sodium soy sauce
1 T. coriander
$1/4$ tsp. curry powder
$1/8$ tsp. pepper
4 bone–in chicken breast halves, skinned

Combine yogurt, lemon juice, soy sauce, coriander, curry powder and pepper in a $1^1/2$ quart shallow baking dish. Turn chicken breasts in sauce to coat all sides. Cover and marinate several hours or overnight in refrigerator. Bake chicken, uncovered, at 375° for 40–45 minutes or until tender, basting frequently with sauce.

*Store spices in a cool
place away from any
direct source of heat,
as the heat will de-
stroy their flavors.
Red spices will
maintain flavor
and color longer
if refrigerated.*

Sesame Ginger Chicken

4 boneless chicken breast halves, skinned
¼ c. low–sodium soy sauce
2 T. water
1 T. dried onion flakes
1 T. sesame seeds
½ tsp. ginger
1 clove garlic, minced

Place chicken in a bowl or plastic bag. Combine soy sauce and remaining ingredients; pour over chicken. Cover or seal and marinate in the refrigerator 4 hours or longer, turning occasionally. Remove chicken from marinade. Grill over medium–high heat for 5 minutes; turn and continue cooking until done.

Yield:
   4 servings
Serving Size:
   1 chicken breast
   half
Preparation Time:
   10 minutes
Marinating Time:
   4 hours
Cooking Time:
   10–15 minutes

Nutrient Analysis per serving:

Calories:	170
Fat:	4.2 gm
Cholesterol:	72 mg
Sodium:	210 mg

Less marinade is needed if you marinate meats by placing them in a tightly sealed plastic bag with its excess air squeezed out.

Sweet & Sour Chicken

Yield:
4 servings

Serving Size:
1 ²/₃ cups

Preparation Time:
20 minutes

Cooking Time:
20 minutes

Nutrient Analysis per serving:

Calories: 430
Fat: 6.9 gm
Cholesterol: 54 mg
Sodium: 213 mg

1 c. brown rice
³/₄ lb. chicken breasts, skinned, boned
    and cut into cubes
1 T. peanut oil
1 c. carrots, sliced
1 garlic clove, minced
1 c. green pepper strips
1 can (8 oz.) chunk pineapple, in juice
1 T. cornstarch
¹/₄ c. low–sodium soy sauce
3 T. brown sugar
3 T. vinegar
¹/₂ tsp. ginger

Cook rice according to package directions. In a large skillet, brown chicken in peanut oil. Add carrots and garlic; stir and cook 1–2 minutes. Add green pepper and pineapple with juice. Combine cornstarch, soy sauce, sugar, vinegar and ginger; add to chicken mixture. Bring to a boil, stirring constantly until sauce thickens. Serve over hot rice.

Chicken Cacciatore

Just wait until you smell this cooking!

4 bone–in chicken breast halves, skinned
1 garlic clove, minced
2 tsp. lemon juice
¼ large onion, sliced
1 c. fresh mushrooms, sliced
2 cans (8 oz. each) tomato sauce
½ tsp. Italian seasoning
1 T. Parmesan cheese, grated

Preheat oven to 350°. Rub garlic on chicken breasts. Place chicken in roasting pan and sprinkle with lemon juice. Layer onion and mushroom slices over chicken. Pour tomato sauce on top and sprinkle with Italian seasoning and cheese. Cover and bake 1 hour. Serve with cooked pasta.

Yield:
 4 servings

Serving Size:
 1 chicken breast
 half with ¼
 of vegetables
 and sauce

Preparation Time:
 10–15 minutes

Cooking Time:
 1 hour

Nutrient Analysis per serving:

Calories: 200
Fat: 3.9 gm
Cholesterol: 74 mg
Sodium: 132 mg

Skinless dark poultry meat has more than twice as much fat as skinless light meat.

Blackened Chicken Breasts

Use this Blackened Spice Mix on chicken, fish and lean beef for a snappy entree.

Yield:
4 servings

Serving Size:
1 chicken breast
half

Preparation Time:
5 minutes

Cooking Time:
15–18 minutes

1 T. paprika
1 tsp. onion powder
1 tsp. garlic powder
1 tsp. cayenne pepper
$^3/_4$ tsp. white pepper
$^3/_4$ tsp. pepper
$^1/_2$ tsp. salt
$^1/_2$ tsp. dried whole thyme
$^1/_2$ tsp. dried whole oregano
4 boneless chicken breast halves, skinned
1 T. oil

**Nutrient Analysis
per serving:**

Calories: 176
Fat: 6.6 gm
Cholesterol: 72 mg
Sodium: 195 mg

Combine first 9 ingredients to make the blackened spice mix. Coat each chicken breast with about 1 teaspoon of spice mix. Store remaining spice mix for another use. In a large, nonstick skillet, cook chicken in hot oil over medium heat. Turn chicken over when first side is browned (about 7 minutes), and cook until done. Serve on a Kaiser roll, garnished with lemon wedges.

You were not born with a preference for salt — you <u>learned</u> it! This means that you "unlearn" it by gradually lowering the amount of salt in your diet. Most people who gradually reduce the amount of salt they eat lose their desire for the salty taste.

166

Tarragon and Wine Poached Chicken

A chicken and mushroom combination delicately flavored with wine and tarragon.

4 boneless chicken breast halves, skinned
¹/₃ lb. fresh mushrooms, sliced
¹/₂ tsp. salt
¹/₂ tsp. dried whole tarragon
¹/₄ tsp. pepper
2 T. fresh parsley, chopped
³/₄ c. dry white wine

Place chicken and mushrooms in a large skillet; sprinkle with salt, tarragon, pepper and parsley. Pour wine over chicken. Cover and simmer for 15 minutes or until chicken is tender. Serve with sauce left from skillet.

Yield:
4 servings

Serving Size:
1 chicken breast half with ¹/₄ of sauce

Preparation Time:
10 minutes

Cooking Time:
15–20 minutes

Nutrient Analysis per serving:

Calories: 181
Fat: 3.2 gm
Cholesterol: 72 mg
Sodium: 363 mg

Taking the skin off of a half breast of roasted chicken reduces the fat from 8 grams to 3 grams, and calories from 195 to 140.

Breast of Chicken Dijon

A popular entree at the Wellshire Inn Restaurant — thanks to Executive Chef Gerard van Mourik for letting us share his recipe.

Yield:
  2 servings

Serving Size:
  1 chicken breast
  half

Preparation Time:
  7 minutes

Cooking Time:
  10 minutes

Nutrient Analysis per serving:

Calories: 229
Fat: 3.6 gm
Cholesterol: 72 mg
Sodium: 163 mg

½ c. white wine
2 shallots, finely diced
1 tsp. dried whole tarragon
1 T. Dijon mustard
1 T. honey
Salt and pepper to taste
2 boneless chicken breast halves, skinned

In a small saucepan, reduce the white wine, shallots and tarragon until half of the liquid is left. Remove from heat and stir in mustard, honey, salt and pepper. Coat chicken with honey–mustard sauce and grill for 5 minutes. Turn chicken and baste with more sauce; cook until done. Serve with extra sauce on the side.

Use a plastic cutting board when cutting chicken, raw meat or fish to prevent harmful bacteria from being spread. Wooden cutting boards may retain bacteria and contaminate other foods.

168

Rosemary Lemon Chicken

1 ½ c. fresh mushrooms, sliced
1 clove garlic, minced
1 T. olive oil
4 boneless chicken breast halves, skinned
2 T. flour
½ tsp. dried whole rosemary
¼ c. lemon juice
¼ c. chicken broth
2 T. parsley, chopped

Yield:
 4 servings

Serving Size:
 1 chicken breast
 half with
 ¼ of sauce

Preparation Time:
 20 minutes

Cooking Time:
 20 minutes

In a large nonstick skillet, sauté mushrooms and garlic in oil for 3–5 minutes. Remove from pan. Combine flour and rosemary; dust chicken with flour mixture and brown on both sides. Add lemon juice and broth to chicken and stir, scraping up any browned bits. Return mushrooms to pan. Cover and simmer for 15 minutes. Garnish with parsley.

*Nutrient Analysis
per serving:*

Calories: 198
Fat: 6.8 gm
Cholesterol: 72 mg
Sodium: 73 mg

Morrocan Stuffed Chicken Breasts

Yield:
4 servings

Serving Size:
1 chicken breast half with ½ cup bulgur

Preparation Time:
20–25 minutes

Cooking Time:
25 minutes

Nutrient Analysis per serving:

Calories: 290
Fat: 7.4 gm
Cholesterol: 72 mg
Sodium: 103 mg

½ c. bulgur or cracked wheat
¼ c. onion, chopped
¼ c. carrot, shredded
¼ c. celery, thinly sliced
1 c. low–sodium chicken broth
4 boneless chicken breast halves, skinned
1 T. oil

SAUCE:
½ c. dry white wine
½ c. low–sodium chicken broth
1 T. fresh parsley, chopped

In a saucepan, combine bulgur, onion, carrot, celery and broth. Bring to a boil. Reduce heat; cover and simmer 15 minutes or until bulgur is done. Cut a pocket in the thickest part of each breast half. Spoon bulgur mixture into each pocket; reserve remaining mixture. Secure pockets with wooden picks. In a large nonstick skillet, cook chicken in oil over medium heat. Turn chicken once during cooking. Cook about 10–15 minutes or until done. Remove picks; place in a shallow serving dish. Sprinkle remaining bulgur mixture over chicken and keep warm. To skillet, add wine and chicken broth. Boil uncovered about 5 minutes or until reduced to ½ cup. Spoon sauce over chicken breasts and garnish with parsley.

Saucy Chicken and New Potatoes

After working all day, mix up this easy dish; then put your feet up and relax while it cooks.

1 c. hot water
1 chicken bouillon cube
4 bone–in chicken breast halves, skinned
2 T. oil
1 medium onion, sliced
1 garlic clove, minced
2 T. flour
1/2 tsp. salt
1/4 tsp. pepper
12 small new potatoes, fresh or canned
1/4 c. dry red wine
Snipped fresh parsley

Dissolve bouillon cube in hot water; set aside. In a large nonstick skillet, sauté chicken breasts in hot oil on both sides until browned. Add onion and garlic; cook 5 minutes or until onion is tender. In a small bowl, combine flour, salt and pepper; slowly stir in bouillon. Pour over browned chicken; add fresh potatoes. Cover and cook slowly about 35 minutes (if using canned potatoes, add them during the last 10 minutes of cooking). Cook until chicken and potatoes are tender. Add wine; heat thoroughly. Garnish with parsley.

Yield:
4 servings

Serving Size:
1 chicken breast half and 3 potatoes

Preparation Time:
25 minutes

Cooking Time:
40 minutes

Nutrient Analysis per serving:

Calories: 332
Fat: 10.2 gm
Cholesterol: 72 mg
Sodium: 656 mg

171

New potatoes contain more moisture and less starch than other mature potatoes. For this reason they will absorb less sauce and dressing, and thus, fewer calories.

Indonesian Chicken in Peanut Sauce

An unusual combination with delightful results.

Yield:
  4 servings

Serving Size:
  1 ⅔ cups

Preparation Time:
  20 minutes

Cooking Time:
  10 minutes

Nutrient Analysis per serving:

Calories: 416
Fat: 15 gm
Cholesterol: 75 mg
Sodium: 516 mg

¼ c. chunky peanut butter

3 T. low–sodium soy sauce

2 T. red wine vinegar

2 T. water

2 tsp. sesame oil

½ tsp. crushed red pepper flakes

1 T. peanut oil

1 lb. chicken meat, cut into 1½-inch strips

1 clove garlic, minced

1 c. green pepper, sliced

1 c. zucchini, julienne sliced

1 c. carrots, julienne sliced

8 oz. eggless spaghettini (thin pasta)

2 c. leaf lettuce, shredded (optional)

In a small bowl combine peanut butter, soy sauce, vinegar, water, sesame oil, and red pepper flakes. Stir until mixture is well blended; set aside. Heat peanut oil in wok. Add chicken and garlic; stir fry for 4–5 minutes. Push chicken up the sides of the wok and add green pepper, zucchini and carrots. Stir–fry until vegetables are crisp yet tender (about 3 minutes). Meanwhile, cook pasta according to package directions; al dente. Toss pasta mixture with peanut sauce. To serve, arrange cooked pasta in peanut sauce on plate and top with shredded lettuce (if desired). Spoon chicken/vegetable mixture on top.

Oven–Fried Italian Chicken

¹/₂ c. lemon juice
1 c. oil–free Italian salad dressing
2 lbs. chicken, cut up and skinned
1 ¹/₂ c. Italian breadcrumbs
¹/₂ tsp. salt
Cooking spray

Mix lemon juice and salad dressing together. Marinate chicken in lemon juice mixture for at least 8 hours or overnight in the refrigerator, turning occasionally. Heat oven to 350°. Mix breadcrumbs and salt. Coat chicken pieces with crumbs and place on foil–covered cookie sheet coated with cooking spray. Bake 1 hour or until tender.

Yield:
4 servings

Serving Size:
¹/₄ of chicken

Preparation Time:
15 minutes

Marinating Time:
8 hours

Cooking Time:
1 hour

Nutrient Analysis per serving:

Calories: 339
Fat: 8.1 gm
Cholesterol: 78 mg
Sodium: 652 mg

Peanut oil is the oil of choice for stir–frying. It can be heated to extremely high temperature before it will begin to smoke.

Broccoli Cashew Chicken

Yield:
    4 servings
Serving Size:
    1-1/3 cups
Preparation Time:
    15 minutes
Cooking Time:
    10–15 minutes

**Nutrient Analysis
per serving:**

Calories: 323
Fat: 14.8 gm
Cholesterol: 72 mg
Sodium: 303 mg

2 T. low-sodium soy sauce

2 tsp. cooking sherry

1 1/2 tsp. sugar

1 1/2 tsp. white wine vinegar

1 tsp. cornstarch

Dash hot pepper sauce

1 T. low-sodium soy sauce

1 tsp. cornstarch

4 boneless chicken breast halves, skinned
    and cut into cubes

1 T. peanut oil, divided

1/2 c. cashew nuts

2 c. broccoli flowerets

1 medium onion, cut in 8 wedges

2 cloves garlic, minced

1/4 tsp. ginger

Combine first 5 ingredients; set aside. Combine 1 tablespoon soy sauce and 1 teaspoon cornstarch in a medium bowl. Add chicken cubes and stir to coat; set aside. Over medium heat, heat half of the oil in wok. Add cashews and stir–fry until brown (about 1 minute). Remove nuts, set aside. Add remaining oil to wok. When oil is hot, add chicken and stir-fry 2–3 minutes until chicken starts to turn opaque. Add broccoli, onion and ginger; continue to stir–fry until broccoli becomes tender. Add reserved cooking sauce and stir–fry until sauce thickens. Add nuts, stir and serve.

Stir–fry meals are a good way of disguising smaller meat portions. Your family won't notice if a variety of colorful vegetables make up the bulk of your stir–fry meal.

Chicken in Orange–
Almond Sauce

**2 lbs. chicken, cut up and skinned
    OR 4 bone–in chicken breasts, skinned**
$\frac{1}{2}$ tsp. salt
2 T. oil
2 T. flour
$\frac{1}{8}$ tsp. cinnamon
Dash of ginger
$\frac{1}{4}$ tsp. salt
1 $\frac{1}{2}$ c. orange juice
$\frac{1}{4}$ c. almonds, sliced
$\frac{1}{3}$ c. raisins

Yield:
    4 servings
Serving Size:
    $\frac{1}{4}$ of chicken
        and sauce
Preparation Time:
    25–30 minutes
Cooking Time:
    55–65 minutes

Preheat oven to 350°. Season chicken pieces with $\frac{1}{2}$ teaspoon salt. Heat oil in a large nonstick skillet; lightly brown the chicken. Arrange browned chicken in a shallow baking dish; set aside. Combine flour, cinnamon, ginger and $\frac{1}{4}$ teaspoon salt; add to drippings in skillet to make a smooth paste. Cook 1 minute. Slowly add orange juice; cook over medium heat, stirring constantly, until mixture is thickened and bubbly. Remove from heat; stir in almonds and raisins. Pour sauce over chicken. Cover and bake for 25 minutes. Then, uncover and continue baking another 30 minutes.

Nutrient Analysis per serving:

Calories: 345
Fat: 14.6 gm
Cholesterol: 72 mg
Sodium: 510 mg

Chicken Curry

If you like curry — you'll love this.

Yield:
4 servings

Serving Size:
¼ of chicken
and sauce

Preparation Time:
10 minutes

Cooking Time:
45 minutes

Nutrient Analysis per serving:

Calories: 244
Fat: 9.2 gm
Cholesterol: 75 mg
Sodium: 290 mg

1 T. margarine
1 medium onion, chopped
1 T. curry powder
1 tsp. ginger
¼ tsp. allspice
¼ tsp. cayenne pepper
¼ tsp. salt
¼ tsp. pepper
1 can (6 oz.) tomato paste
½ c. plain nonfat yogurt
2 lb. chicken pieces, skinned
1 c. chicken broth (optional)

In a large nonstick skillet, melt margarine and sauté onion; add spices, tomato paste and yogurt. Stir until sauce is smooth. Add chicken pieces, spooning sauce over chicken to coat pieces with sauce; cover and simmer about 45 minutes or until chicken is tender. (This recipe makes a dry type chicken. If a sauce is desired, add 1 cup chicken broth during simmering.)

Mediterranean Chicken with Mushrooms

2 lbs. chicken, cut up and skinned
1 lb. fresh mushrooms, halved
1 tsp. salt, divided
1/4 tsp. pepper
1 can (14 1/2 oz.) tomatoes, chopped
1/2 c. onion, chopped
1 garlic clove, minced
2 tsp. dried whole basil
1 bay leaf
3 medium zucchini, cut into 2-inch strips
1 green pepper, cut into strips
2 T. flour
Parmesan cheese, grated (optional)

Yield:
4 servings

Serving Size:
1/4 of chicken
and vegetables

Preparation Time:
15–20 minutes

Cooking Time:
50–60 minutes

Preheat oven to 425°. Sprinkle chicken with 1/2 teaspoon salt and the pepper; place in a 13x9x2-inch pan; bake 10 minutes. Reduce oven temperature to 350°. In a large bowl, combine tomatoes, onion, garlic, basil, bay leaf, zucchini, green pepper, mushrooms and 1/2 tsp. salt; stir well. Pour mixture over chicken; cover and bake about 40–50 minutes or until tender. Remove chicken from pan; set aside. Remove 1/2 cup vegetable liquid from pan; stir in flour until smooth. Add back to vegetables in pan and cook over medium heat until sauce thickens. Pour vegetable sauce over chicken and sprinkle with Parmesan cheese.

Nutrient Analysis per serving:

Calories: 242
Fat: 7.3 gm
Cholesterol: 76 mg
Sodium: 787 mg

Turkey Piccata

Yield:
4 servings

Serving Size:
4 ounces

Preparation Time:
15 minutes

Cooking Time:
6–10 minutes

1 lb. boneless fresh turkey breast slices
¼ c. flour
1 T. olive oil
½ c. dry white wine
¼ c. lemon juice
2 T. capers

Lightly coat turkey slices with flour. Heat oil in a medium–size nonstick skillet. Cook turkey 1½ to 2 minutes on each side or until lightly browned. Remove to platter and keep warm. Add the wine and lemon juice to the skillet and bring to a boil, scraping up any brown bits. Add capers. Pour the sauce over turkey, and serve immediately.

**Nutrient Analysis
per serving:**

Calories: 217
Fat: 6.3 gm
Cholesterol: 59 mg
Sodium: 62 mg

Skinless turkey has about one–third less fat than skinless chicken. No wonder it's a part of healthy eating.

MEATS

MEATS

Tremendous Tenderloin Steaks

So tender it will melt in your mouth.

¹/₄ c. red wine
¹/₄ c. low–sodium soy sauce
¹/₄ tsp. pepper
¹/₄ tsp. dried whole thyme
¹/₈ tsp. hot sauce
¹/₈ tsp. garlic powder
4 (6 oz. each) beef tenderloin steaks

Combine first 6 ingredients; mix well. Place steaks in a shallow dish; pour wine mixture over top. Cover and refrigerate 2 hours, turning occasionally. Remove steaks from marinade and grill over medium–hot coals to desired doneness.

Yield:
4 servings

Serving Size:
6 ounces

Preparation Time:
5 minutes

Marinating Time:
2 hours

Cooking Time:
10–15 minutes

Nutrient Analysis per serving:

Calories: 283
Fat: 11.6 gm
Cholesterol: 107 mg
Sodium: 229 mg

Beef is leaner than ever and easily fits into healthy eating. The leanest cuts of beef are called "The Skinniest Six," they are: eye of round, round tip roast, top loin (strip steak), top, tenderloin and top sirloin.

Glazed London Broil

Marinating tenderizes this lean cut of meat and leaves it with a light oriental flavor.

Yield:
6 servings

Serving Size:
5 ounces

Preparation Time:
10 minutes

Marinating Time:
6 hours

Cooking Time:
6–8 minutes

Nutrient Analysis per serving:

Calories: 317
Fat: 16 gm
Cholesterol: 81 mg
Sodium: 232 mg

2 lbs. flank steak
1 tsp. unseasoned meat tenderizer
2 T. dry sherry
2 T. low–sodium soy sauce
1 ½ T. honey
¼ tsp. ginger

Pierce surface of steak at 1-inch intervals with fork. Combine remaining ingredients and pour over steak. Marinate in a covered container for at least 6 hours in the refrigerator, turning several times. Broil 6 inches from heat for 3 minutes on each side. Cut beef diagonally across the grain; serve warm.

When selecting meat — think cheap! Cuts of meat are priced by the amount of marbling (fat in the meat fibers) they contain. USDA Select cuts are leaner than Prime or Choice cuts, and should cost you less.

Oriental Pepper Steak

1 lb. beef tip round steak
1 T. cornstarch
¼ tsp. ginger
¼ c. low–sodium soy sauce
1 T. peanut oil
3 medium green peppers, cut into
    1-inch squares
1 small onion, chopped
1 clove garlic, minced
½ c. water
2 medium tomatoes, cut into wedges
4 c. cooked rice

Yield:
4 servings
Serving Size:
1 ⅔ cups
Preparation Time:
20 minutes
Cooking Time:
10 minutes

**Nutrient Analysis
per serving:**

Calories: 431
Fat: 10.6 gm
Cholesterol: 69 mg
Sodium: 239 mg

Slice beef diagonally across the grain into very thin slices. (Tip: meat will slice easier if frozen for 1 hour). In a small bowl, combine cornstarch and ginger; add soy sauce and stir. Pour soy sauce mixture over beef and stir. Heat oil in wok over medium–high heat. Add beef to wok and stir–fry until brown; remove from pan. Reduce heat and add peppers, onion, garlic and water to wok; cook 4–5 minutes. Stir in meat and tomatoes; heat through. Serve with rice.

Trimming the fat from a 3–ounce piece of sirloin steak before broiling lowers the amount of fat from 15 grams to 6 grams, and calories from 240 to 150.

Durango Short Ribs

A one–pot meal that requires a tossed salad to make a feast.

Yield:
8 servings

Serving Size:
1 1/2 cups

Preparation Time:
10 minutes

Cooking Time:
2 hours, 20 minutes

Nutrient Analysis per serving:

Calories: 389
Fat: 15.9 gm
Cholesterol: 79 mg
Sodium: 219 mg

3 lbs. lean boneless beef short ribs
2 medium onions, sliced
1 can (15 oz.) tomato sauce
1 c. water
1/4 c. brown sugar, packed
1/4 c. vinegar
1 tsp. dry mustard
1 tsp. Worcestershire Sauce
1/2 tsp. salt
2 c. linguine noodles, uncooked
1 c. water

In a large nonstick skillet, brown meat; drain fat. Add onions to meat and continue to cook 1 more minute. Blend together tomato sauce, water, brown sugar, vinegar, dry mustard, Worcestershire Sauce and salt. Pour mixture over meat. Cover and simmer for 2 hours or until meat is tender. Skim off fat; stir in uncooked noodles and second cup of water. Cover and cook, stirring occasionally, for 15–20 minutes more, or until noodles are tender.

When sautéing or frying, make sure your cooking oil is hot before adding ingredients. Foods soak up cool oil faster than hot oil. One extra tablespoon of oil absorbed by foods adds 100 calories to the total.

184

Smokey Beef Brisket

2 T. liquid smoke
2 tsp. celery seed
1 tsp. garlic powder
1 tsp. onion powder
1 tsp. Worcestershire sauce
3 lb. lean brisket
$\frac{1}{2}$ tsp. salt
$\frac{1}{2}$ tsp. fresh ground pepper
1 c. bottled barbeque sauce

Yield:
  8 servings
Serving Size:
  4 ounces
Preparation Time:
  10 minutes
Marinating Time:
  6–10 hours
Cooking Time:
  5 hours

Mix liquid smoke, celery seed, garlic powder, onion powder and Worcestershire sauce. Rub both sides of brisket with mixture; place in a covered dish and marinate overnight in the refrigerator. To cook, preheat oven to 300°. Sprinkle brisket with salt and pepper; cover with foil and bake for 4 hours. Add barbeque sauce and bake uncovered for another hour, basting occasionally.

Nutrient Analysis
per serving:

Calories: 199
Fat: 6.1 gm
Cholesterol: 66 mg
Sodium: 467 mg

There are no "good" or "bad' foods, only bad diets. In other words, any food can be a part of a healthful eating plan, at least occasionally.

San Luis Barbequed Beans

*The nutritional benefits of beans are endless.
Introduce your family to more beans
with this popular casserole.*

Yield:
8 servings

Serving Size:
1 ¼ cups

Preparation Time:
20 minutes

Cooking Time:
1 hour

**Nutrient Analysis
per serving:**

Calories: 369
Fat: 6.7 gm
Cholesterol: 32 mg
Sodium: 220 mg

¾ **lb. lean ground beef**
¾ **c. onion, chopped**
½ **c. celery, chopped**
2 **cans (15 oz. each) fat–free baked beans**
1 **can (15 oz.) kidney beans, rinsed and drained**
1 **can (15 oz.) butter or lima beans, rinsed
   and drained**
½ **c. catsup**
⅓ **c. brown sugar, packed**
2 **T. red wine vinegar**
1 **tsp. dry mustard**

Preheat oven to 350 °. In a large nonstick skillet brown beef, adding onion and celery during the last 4 minutes of the browning process. Stir frequently. Drain fat. Add beans to meat mixture. In a separate bowl mix together catsup, sugar, vinegar and mustard. Fold sauce into meat and beans,being careful not to crush beans. Pour mixture into a 2–quart casserole dish and bake for l hour.

*Increase the fiber in
your diet <u>gradually</u>.
Too much fiber too
fast can cause gas,
cramps, diarrhea
and discouragement.*

Old-Timer's Beef Stew

*A crockpot stew that will
fill your home with a wonderful smell.*

2 lbs. lean top round steak, cut into
   1-inch cubes
$1/4$ c. flour
1 T. oil
3 lbs. frozen or fresh stew vegetables
1 c. beef broth
1 T. dried parsley flakes
3 cloves garlic, minced
1 tsp. Worcestershire sauce
$1/2$ tsp. dried whole thyme or marjoram
$1/4$ tsp. salt
$1/4$ tsp. pepper

Yield:
6 servings
Serving Size:
1 $1/2$ cups
Preparation Time:
20 minutes
Cooking Time:
8–10 hours

*Nutrient Analysis
per serving:*

Calories: 369
Fat: 11.8 gm
Cholesterol: 93 mg
Sodium: 490 mg

Combine meat and flour in a zip–top plastic bag; close bag and shake well. Heat oil in a large nonstick skillet over high heat. Add flour–coated meat and cook until browned, stirring often. Place browned meat, stew vegetables and remaining ingredients into crockpot. Stir just enough to mix spices. Cover and cook on LOW for 8–10 hours (HIGH: 4–5 hours).

*Stew vegetables can
be found frozen or
sometimes, fresh
combinations, in the
produce department.*

Simply
COLORADO

Rancher's Meat Loaf

*The rich flavor of meatloaf with the
nutrition of oatmeal.*

Yield:
  8 servings

Serving Size:
  1 slice

Preparation Time:
  10 minutes

Cooking Time:
  1 hour

**Nutrient Analysis
per serving:**

Calories: 180
Fat: 9.5 gm
Cholesterol: 71 mg
Sodium: 218 mg

1 c. tomato juice
³/4 c. regular oats, uncooked
1 egg
¹/4 c. onion, chopped
¹/4 c. green pepper, chopped
1 T. Worcestershire sauce
¹/2 tsp. salt
¹/2 tsp. dry mustard
¹/4 tsp. garlic powder
¹/4 tsp. pepper
1 ¹/2 lbs. lean ground beef
Chopped parsley and oats, for garnish

Preheat oven to 350°. Combine all ingredients
except for ground meat and garnish; mix well.
Add meat and mix thoroughly. Press into 9x5-
inch loaf pan; garnish and bake 1 hour. Let stand
5 minutes before serving.

*Cholesterol is a
fat–like substance
found only in animal
products such as egg
yolks, meat, poultry,
fish and dairy pro-
ducts. Foods of plant
origin, such as fruits,
vegetables, grains
and nuts, have no
cholesterol.*

Pizza Burgers

*Healthier and more fun
than a regular cheeseburger.*

1 lb. lean ground beef
½ c. celery, diced
2 T. Worcestershire sauce
½ tsp. Italian seasoning
⅓ c. tomato sauce
4 slices (⅔ oz. each) sharp reduced–fat
   Cheddar cheese

Yield:
   4 servings
Serving Size:
   4 ounces
Preparation Time:
   10 minutes
Cooking Time:
   10 minutes

Combine meat, celery, onion, Worcestershire sauce and Italian seasoning; mix well and shape into 4 patties. Grill patties over medium–hot coals for 5 minutes on each side or until done. During the last minutes of cooking, brush the top of each patty with tomato sauce and top with a slice of cheese.

*Nutrient Analysis
per serving:*

Calories: 290
Fat: 16 gm
Cholesterol: 85 mg
Sodium: 567 mg

189

Vegetable Burgers

*Get out of your grilling rut
and try this tasty number.*

Yield:
  4 servings

Serving Size:
  1 patty

Preparation Time:
  10–15 minutes

Cooking Time:
  15 minutes

**Nutrient Analysis
per serving:**

Calories: 213
Fat: 7.6 gm
Cholesterol: 42 mg
Sodium: 45 mg

³/₄ c. potatoes, shredded
¹/₂ lb. lean ground beef
¹/₃ c. mushrooms, finely chopped
2 T. onion, minced
¹/₈ tsp. garlic powder
¹/₈ tsp. lemon–pepper seasoning

Place potatoes between paper towels and **squeeze until barely moist**; combine with remaining ingredients. Shape into 4 patties. Grill over medium–hot coals 7–8 minutes on each side or until done. (To oven broil, place patties on broiler pan coated with cooking spray. Broil 6 inches from heat for about 8 minutes on each side.)

Buffaloaf

*Go ahead, try something new for dinner
— like buffalo!*

1 lb. lean ground buffalo
²/₃ c. regular oats, uncooked
¹/₃ c. commercial barbeque sauce
1 egg
¹/₄ c. onion, chopped
¹/₄ c. green pepper, chopped
1 T. dried parsley flakes
2 tsp. Worcestershire sauce
Cooking spray

Preheat oven to 350°. Combine all ingredients and place in a 9x5x3-inch pan coated with cooking spray. Bake for 45–50 minutes or until done.

Yield:
  4 servings
Serving Size:
  4 ounces
Preparation Time:
  10–15 minutes
Cooking Time:
  45–50 minutes

Nutrient Analysis per serving:

Calories:	199
Fat:	9 gm
Cholesterol:	87 mg
Sodium:	229 mg

Buffalo is naturally flavorful and lean. Ground buffalo can be used in many recipes in place of ground beef.

Lemon Ginger Lamb Chops

Yield:
4 servings

Serving Size:
2 lamb chops

Preparation Time:
5 minutes

Cooking Time:
10–15 minutes

Nutrient Analysis per serving:

Calories: 290
Fat: 7.4 gm
Cholesterol: 85 mg
Sodium: 215 mg

$^{1}/_{2}$ c. pineapple juice
$^{1}/_{2}$ c. brown sugar, packed
2 tsp. minced fresh ginger OR
   1 tsp. dry ground ginger
2 tsp. grated lemon peel
Salt and pepper to taste
8 lamb chops, 1-inch thick

In saucepan, combine pineapple juice, brown sugar, ginger, lemon peel, salt and pepper. Cook over medium heat until sugar dissolves. Brush both sides of lamb chops with glaze and arrange chops on broiler rack. Broil 6 inches from heat for 5–7 minutes each side, or to desired doneness. Brush frequently with glaze.

When grating or zesting lemon, lime or orange peel, grate extra and store it in the freezer.

Royal Gorge
Roast Rack of Lamb

*Simple, yet elegant. Save this for
someone you really want to impress.*

**1 rack of lamb (about 2 lbs., 12 ribs),
    well–trimmed**
1 ¹/₂ tsp. stone–ground mustard
¹/₃ c. dry breadcrumbs
2 T. fresh parsley, chopped
¹/₂ tsp. dried whole rosemary leaves
¹/₄ tsp. pepper

Preheat oven to 375°. On roasting rack in
shallow baking pan, place lamb roast, meaty
side up. Spread mustard over meat. Combine
bread crumbs, parsley, rosemary and pepper. Pat
bread crumb mixture over mustard. Roast until
desired doneness; 140° for rare, 150–155° for
medium, or 160° for medium–well. Let roast
stand for 10 minutes before carving.

Yield:
    6 servings
Serving Size:
    2 ribs
Preparation Time:
    5–10 minutes
Cooking Time:
    1 hour, 10 minutes

**Nutrient Analysis
per serving:**

Calories: 214
Fat: 10.6 gm
Cholesterol: 85 mg
Sodium: 114 mg

Spicy Grilled Chops

A barbeque sensation!

Yield:
4 servings

Serving Size:
4 ounces

Preparation Time:
5 minutes

Marinating Time:
1 hour

Cooking Time:
8–10 minutes

Nutrient Analysis per serving:

Calories: 249
Fat: 12.2 gm
Cholesterol: 80 mg
Sodium: 130 mg

¼ c. thick and chunky hot salsa
2 T. water
2 T. orange marmalade
¼ tsp. seasoned salt
4 boneless center cut pork loin chops,
    ½-inch thick, trimmed (about 1 lb.)

In a small bowl, combine salsa, water, marmalade and salt; blend well. Place pork chops in plastic bag or non–metal baking dish. Pour marinade mixture over pork, turning to coat. Seal bag or cover dish; marinate 1 hour, turning pork chops several times. Remove pork chops from marinade, reserving marinade. Place chops on grill 4–6 inches from medium–hot coals. Grill about 4 minutes per side, basting with reserved marinade.

Pork Chops in Apple Juice

4 boneless center cut pork loin chops
   (about 1 lb.)
Cooking spray
¼ tsp. dried whole sage
Salt and pepper to taste
1 c. apple juice
¼ c. raisins

Preheat oven to 350°. Trim any excess fat from pork chops; brown in a nonstick skillet coated with cooking spray. Arrange in baking dish (single layer if possible). Sprinkle chops with sage, salt and pepper; cover with apple juice. Cover and bake about 1 hour or until meat is tender. Add raisins during last half hour of baking.

Hint: Can be simmered in covered pan on stove if preferred over baking.

Yield:
   4 servings
Serving Size:
   4 ounces
Preparation Time:
   10 minutes
Cooking Time:
   1 hour

*Nutrient Analysis
per serving:*

Calories: 276
Fat: 12.8 gm
Cholesterol: 80 mg
Sodium: 214 mg

The National Pork Producers Council recently revised their cooking recommendations for lean pork to an internal temperature of 160° for medium doneness. At this temperature, pork will be tender, juicy and slightly pink in the middle.

Sesame Pork with Broccoli

After a weekend in the mountains, this makes a quick, one–dish Sunday supper.

Yield:
4 servings

Serving Size:
1 ¹/₂ cups

Preparation Time:
5 minutes

Cooking Time:
10–15 minutes

Nutrient Analysis per serving:

Calories: 318
Fat: 15.3 gm
Cholesterol: 71 mg
Sodium: 418 mg

1 can (14 ¹/₂ oz.) chicken broth
2 T. cornstarch
1 T. low–sodium soy sauce
4 green onions, sliced
1 lb. pork tenderloin, trimmed
1 T. peanut oil
1 clove garlic, minced
1 ¹/₂ lb. fresh broccoli, flowerets
2 T. sesame seeds, lightly toasted

In a small bowl, combine chicken broth, cornstarch and soy sauce; blend well. Stir in green onions; set aside. Cut pork tenderloin into bite–sized pieces. Heat oil in wok. Add pork and garlic; stir–fry for 4–5 minutes or until pork is done. Remove pork; keep warm. Add broccoli and broth mixture to wok. Cover and simmer over low heat for 6 minutes. Add cooked pork; cook just until mixture is hot, stirring frequently. Sprinkle with sesame seeds; serve immediately.

A serving of broccoli (about 1 cup) contains more vitamin C than an orange — more than enough to meet the Recommended Dietary Allowance.

Cinnamon Grilled Pork Tenderloin

The surprising kick of cinnamon goes well with this mild–flavored meat.

3 T. low–sodium soy sauce
3 T. cooking sherry
1 T. brown sugar
½ T. honey
½ tsp. garlic salt
½ tsp. cinnamon
2 (¾ lb. each) pork tenderloin

Yield:
  6 servings
Serving Size:
  4 ounces
Preparation Time:
  5 minutes
Marinating Time:
  2–6 hours
Cooking Time:
  15–20 minutes

Combine first 6 ingredients in a large zip–top plastic bag. Add tenderloins and refrigerate no more than 6 hours (the flavor of the meat is lost if it is marinated too long). Remove tenderloins from marinade and insert a meat thermometer. Grill tenderloins over hot coals for 12–15 minutes or until thermometer reaches 160°, turning while grilling. Serve with an oriental rice dish and spinach salad.

Nutrient Analysis per serving:

Calories: 213
Fat: 5.4 gm
Cholesterol: 104 mg
Sodium: 348 mg

Marinades serve two functions: to flavor and to tenderize. A tender cut of meat, such as pork tenderloin, is often marinated to enhance flavor. A less tender cut of meat, such as sirloin, needs marinating for tenderness.

Krautburgers

Anyone with a German background will recognize this lean version of an old favorite. Freeze them ahead and pack them for lunch.

Yield:
16 servings

Serving Size:
1 krautburger

Preparation Time:
25–30 minutes

Rising Time:
10 minutes

Cooking Time:
20 minutes

Nutrient Analysis per serving:

Calories: 225
Fat: 5.7 gm
Cholesterol: 23 mg
Sodium: 423 mg

1 lb. lean ground beef
1 medium onion, chopped
$^{1}/_{2}$ head of cabbage, shredded
$^{1}/_{2}$ envelope ($^{1}/_{2}$ oz.) onion soup mix
Pepper to taste
2 loaves frozen bread dough, thawed
Cooking spray

Preheat oven to 350°. Brown ground beef and onion in a large nonstick skillet; drain fat. Add cabbage and cook 5 minutes longer. Stir soup mix and pepper into ground beef and cabbage mixture. Set aside. Roll one loaf of bread dough into a 16x8-inch rectangle, then cut into eight 4-inch squares. Spoon mixture into center of each square, bring up diagonal points, pinching edges closed. Let *Krautburgers* rise on a cookie sheet coated with cooking spray for about 10 minutes. Bake for 20 minutes or until brown. If desired, brush tops of warm rolls with margarine. Repeat process with second loaf of bread and remaining mixture.

MEXICAN

MEXICAN

Salsa Fresca

3 c. tomato, diced
1 fresh jalapeno pepper, seeded and diced
1 can (4 oz.) chopped green chilies
1/2 c. green onions, sliced
1/4 c. fresh cilantro, chopped
2–3 T. fresh lime juice
1 tsp. chili powder
1 tsp. dried whole oregano
1 tsp. garlic salt

Yield:
   3 cups
   6 servings
Serving Size:
   1/2 cup
Preparation Time:
   20 minutes
Chilling Time:
   30 minutes

Combine all ingredients in a large mixing bowl; refrigerate 30 minutes to allow flavors to blend.

Nutrient Analysis per serving:

Calories: 22
Fat: 0 gm
Cholesterol: 0 mg
Sodium: 626 mg

Fresh cilantro can be found in the produce section of most supermarkets; it may be labeled as Chinese parsley. Cilantro doesn't hold up well under long periods of high heat, so add it toward the end of cooking for the best flavor.

Oven Tortilla Chips

Serve with salsa — these chips make a great snack with almost <u>no</u> fat.

Yield:
  72 chips
  12 servings

Serving Size:
  6 chips

Preparation Time:
  3–5 minutes

Cooking Time:
  8–10 minutes

12 corn tortillas
Water or cooking spray
Onion or garlic salt to taste (optional)

Preheat oven to 400°. Cut each tortilla into 6 wedges. Place wedges on a baking sheet and spray with water or cooking spray. Sprinkle with onion or garlic salt. Bake 6–8 or until crisp. (Avoid browning or they will start to taste burnt.) Cool and serve with salsa. Store in airtight container.

Variation: Top with sugar and cinnamon and serve as a dessert.

Nutrient Analysis per serving:

Calories: 68
Fat: 1 gm
Cholesterol: 0 mg
Sodium: 53 mg

*Commercial tortilla chips contain **four times more fat** than our recipe.*

Five–Layer Mexican Dip

You'll find that they won't leave this dip alone.

1 can (15 oz.) fat–free refried beans
¹/₂ c. mild salsa
¹/₂ ripe avocado
¹/₂ c. plain nonfat yogurt
2 c. lettuce, shredded
¹/₂ c. tomatoes, chopped
1 oz. sharp reduced–fat Cheddar cheese,
  shredded

In a small bowl, mix together beans and salsa. In a separate bowl, blend together the avocado and yogurt. In a shallow serving dish, layer ingredients beginning with the bean mixture. Top with avocado sauce, then cover with lettuce, tomato and cheese. Serve with *Oven Tortilla Chips.*

Yield:
  5 cups
  20 servings

Serving Size:
  ¹/₄ cup

Preparation Time:
  15 minutes

Nutrient Analysis per serving:

Calories: 45
Fat: 1 gm
Cholesterol: 0 mg
Sodium: 36 mg

*To get more cheese flavor for less fat, use **sharp** Cheddar cheese and cut down on the amount of cheese you use. Grate it and put it on top of a casserole so that it's visible — don't hide it inside.*

Santa Fe Beans

Why buy refried beans containing lard when Santa Fe beans taste so good and have no added fat?

Yield:
　4 cups
　8 servings

Serving Size:
　¹/₂ cup

Preparation Time:
　10 minutes

Nutrient Analysis per serving:

Calories:　212
Fat:　1 gm
Cholesterol: 0 mg
Sodium:　379 mg

1 can (15 oz.) kidney beans
1 can (15 oz.) navy beans
1 can (15 oz.) pinto beans OR 6 c. same mixture of beans, cooked
³/₄ c. onion, minced
3 cloves garlic, minced
2 ¹/₄ tsp. chili powder
1 ¹/₂ tsp. cumin
³/₄ tsp. salt
1 can (4 oz.) diced green chilies

Drain canned beans; rinse with water (to wash away added sodium). Place beans and remaining ingredients in a blender or food processor; process until a little chunky (not completely smooth). Serve as a bean dip or filler for burritos and tacos.

Store–bought refried beans are usually made with lard, a highly saturated animal fat. A better choice would be fat–free or vegetarian refried beans, which are made with no fat or polyunsaturated vegetable fat.

204

Alamosa Posole

Cooking spray
1 c. onion, chopped
2 cloves garlic, minced
2 cans (15½ oz. each) yellow hominy, drained
2 c. tomatoes, chopped
1 can (4 oz.) chopped green chilies
1 tsp. chili powder
½ tsp. cumin
¼ tsp. pepper
½ c. (2 oz.) sharp reduced–fat Cheddar
  cheese, shredded

Yield:
  8 servings
Serving Size:
  ½ cup
Preparation Time:
  15 minutes
Cooking Time:
  30 minutes

*Nutrient Analysis
per serving:*

Calories: 116
Fat: 1.3 gm
Cholesterol: 0 mg
Sodium: 455 mg

Preheat oven to 350°. Coat a nonstick skillet with cooking spray; place over medium heat. Add onion and garlic; sauté until tender. Add hominy, tomatoes, green chilies, chili powder, cumin and pepper; mix thoroughly. Spoon mixture into a 2–quart casserole dish coated with cooking spray; bake, uncovered for 25 minutes. Add cheese and bake 5 minutes more, or until cheese melts.

Posole is a popular southwestern dish containing hominy (skinned white corn kernels). Hominy is slightly sweet with a firm texture.

Green Chili Squash

1 medium onion, chopped
1 T. oil
5 c. zucchini, sliced
1 pkg. (16 oz.) frozen corn
1 can (4 oz.) chopped green chilies
¼ c. water
Salt to taste

In a large, nonstick skillet, sauté onion in oil. When onions are soft, add zucchini, corn, green chilies, water and salt. Cover and cook over low heat 10–15 minutes, or until tender.

Yield:
8 servings

Serving Size:
²/₃ cup

Preparation Time:
5 minutes

Cooking Time:
15–20 minutes

Nutrient Analysis per serving:

Calories: 99
Fat: 2.4 gm
Cholesterol: 0 mg
Sodium: 208 mg

Hot peppers contain oils that can burn your eyes, lips and skin; protect yourself by wearing plastic gloves when working with them. If you don't have plastic gloves, try using a plastic bag.

Black Bean Tostadas

4 corn tortillas
Cold water
**1 can (15 oz.) black beans with chili spices
(or add ¼ tsp. chili powder and ¼ tsp.
cumin to regular black beans)**
1 ½ c. lettuce, shredded
**½ c. (2 oz.) reduced–fat Monterey Jack
cheese, shredded**
1 small avocado, peeled, pitted and sliced
1 large tomato, diced
1 c. salsa

Preheat oven to 350°. Dip tortillas in water; drain on paper towels. Place tortillas on rack in oven and bake for 15 minutes or until crisp. Remove from oven and cool. Place beans in a medium saucepan; cook until thoroughly heated. With the back of a spoon, mash about half of the beans on the side of the saucepan. (If beans are too thick, add a little water.) To assemble each tostada, spread a tortilla with ¼ of bean mixture. Cover with ¼ each of lettuce, cheese, avocado and tomato; drizzle with salsa.

Yield:
4 servings

Serving Size:
1 tostada

Preparation Time:
15–20 minutes

Cooking Time:
15 minutes

Nutrient Analysis per serving:

Calories: 324
Fat: 8.8 gm
Cholesterol: 0 mg
Sodium: 383 mg

Summer Siesta Salad

Enjoy this colorful salad, then lean back and let the summer and the cool mountain air lull you to sleep.

Yield:
  4 servings

Serving Size:
  1 salad

Preparation Time:
  20 minutes

Cooking Time:
  20 minutes

Nutrient Analysis per serving:

Calories: 279
Fat: 8.7 gm
Cholesterol: 79 mg
Sodium: 362 mg

2 c. fresh spinach, torn
$^1\!/_2$ c. green onions, sliced
12 cherry tomatoes, halved
1 can (12 oz.) whole kernel corn, drained
$^1\!/_2$ tsp. chili powder
$^1\!/_4$ tsp. cumin
$^1\!/_4$ tsp. garlic powder
1 lb. pork tenderloin, cut into $^1\!/_4$-inch slices
1 T. olive oil
$^1\!/_2$ c. orange juice
2 T. lime juice

In a large bowl, combine spinach, onion, tomatoes and corn; set aside. In medium bowl, combine chili powder, cumin and garlic powder. Add pork and toss to coat. In nonstick skillet, heat oil over high heat. Sauté pork until golden brown; stir in orange and lime juices. Spoon pork mixture over vegetables; toss gently to coat.

Green Chili Soup

*Nothing like traditional chili, this soup is
a favorite of Mexican food lovers.*

Cooking spray

1 medium onion, chopped

2 cloves garlic, minced

$\frac{1}{2}$ tsp. cumin

$\frac{1}{4}$ tsp. pepper

$\frac{1}{8}$ tsp. dried whole oregano

3 medium boiling potatoes, cleaned and cut
into small cubes

1 can (7 oz.) chopped green chilies

1 can (49 $\frac{1}{2}$ oz.) chicken broth (about 6 cups)

3 oz. reduced–fat Monterey Jack cheese,
shredded

Coat a 2–quart saucepan with cooking spray;
add onion and garlic and sauté over medium
heat for about 5 minutes until onion wilts. Stir in
cumin and pepper; continue to cook 2–3
minutes or until onion starts to show signs of
browning. Add oregano, potatoes, green chilies
and chicken broth. Bring to a boil; cover and
simmer 45 minutes. Serve hot with cheese
sprinkled evenly over each serving.

Yield:
9 cups
6 servings

Serving Size:
1 $\frac{1}{2}$ cup

Preparation Time:
20 minutes

Cooking Time:
45 minutes

*Nutrient Analysis
per serving:*

Calories: 162
Fat: 7.2 gm
Cholesterol: 13 mg
Sodium: 541 mg

*Instead of margarine,
butter or oil, use non-
stick cooking sprays.
Margarine and oil
provide 100–120
calories per table-
spoon. There are
only 6 calories per
2 $\frac{1}{2}$ seconds spray
of cooking spray.*

Mexican Cornbread

*Served with a hot bowl of Gringo Chili, there's
nothing better after a day of cross–country skiing.*

Yield:
   12 servings

Serving Size:
   3 ¼ x 3-inch piece

Preparation Time:
   5–10 minutes

Cooking Time:
   35–40 minutes

**Nutrient Analysis
per serving:**

Calories: 158
Fat: 2.4 gm
Cholesterol: 10 mg
Sodium: 442 mg

1 ½ c. cornmeal
¾ tsp. salt
½ tsp. baking soda
1 c. low–fat buttermilk
2 egg whites
1 egg
1 can (16½ oz.) cream–style corn
1 c. sharp reduced–fat Cheddar cheese, grated
1 large onion, chopped
1 clove garlic, minced
1 can (4 oz.) chopped green chilies
2 T. margarine, melted
Cooking spray

Preheat oven to 350°. Combine cornmeal, salt
and baking soda. Stir in buttermilk and remaining ingredients. Spoon into a 13x9x2-inch
baking dish coated with cooking spray and
sprinkled with cornmeal. Bake 45 minutes or
until wooden pick inserted in center comes out
clean. Let cool 5 minutes before serving.

*To lower the
cholesterol in your
recipes, substitute
two egg whites for
each whole egg that
you delete.*

Grilled Fajitas

Simply stated, "These are the best fajitas you'll ever taste."

1 c. oil–free Italian dressing
1 can (4 oz.) diced green chilies
1 ½ lb. flank steak
8 flour tortillas
1 c. lettuce, shredded
½ c. tomato, diced
⅓ c. sharp reduced–fat Cheddar cheese, shredded
Hot sauce

Yield:
  8 servings
Serving Size:
  1 fajita
Preparation Time:
  15–20 minutes
Cooking Time:
  10 minutes

Combine dressing and green chilies. Pour mixture over flank steak and marinate in a covered container for at least 6 hours in the refrigerator, turning occasionally. Grill flank steak 3–4 minutes per side until done. Slice steak diagonally across the grain into thin strips. Assemble fajitas by placing a few pieces of meat on a warmed flour tortilla; top with lettuce, tomato and cheese. Sprinkle with hot sauce (if desired) and roll up.

Nutrient Analysis per serving:

Calories: 249
Fat: 9.6 gm
Cholesterol: 34 mg
Sodium: 335 mg

Variation: Substitute 4 chicken breasts (skinned and deboned) for flank steak for chicken fajitas (205 calories, 3.4 gm fat, 40 mg cholesterol, 336 mg sodium).

Chili Relleno Casserole

If you like Chili Rellenos, but don't have the time or the inclination to make them — this is for you.

Yield:
6 servings

Serving Size:
1 cup

Preparation Time:
20 minutes

Cooking Time:
30 minutes

Nutrient Analysis per serving:

Calories: 237
Fat: 1.7 gm
Cholesterol: 0 mg
Sodium: 867 mg

^{2}/$_3$ c. rice, uncooked
1 can (8 oz.) tomato sauce
^{1}/$_4$ c. green onion, sliced
^{3}/$_4$ tsp. garlic powder
1 tsp. dried whole oregano
1 can (16 oz.) fat–free refried beans
1 can (10 oz.) diced green chilies, drained
^{3}/$_4$ c. sharp reduced–fat Cheddar cheese, shredded

Preheat oven to 350°. Cook rice according to package direction. Combine tomato sauce, onions, garlic powder and oregano; set aside. Coat a 1^1/$_2$-quart casserole dish with cooking spray. Mix beans and rice together. Spread half of the bean/rice mixture in bottom of casserole dish; layer with chopped chilies and ^{1}/$_2$ cup shredded cheese. Cover with remaining bean/rice mixture; pour tomato sauce over top. Bake for 25 minutes. Sprinkle with remaining ^{1}/$_4$ cup shredded cheese and heat 5 minutes or until cheese melts.

Cortez Chicken Enchiladas

Another delectable variation of the Mexican enchilada. Use canned chicken to simplify this dish even further.

½ c. onion, chopped

½ c. green pepper, chopped

1 can (4 oz.) chopped green chilies

½ c. chicken broth

2 c. canned green chili enchilada sauce, divided

½ T. chili powder

1 tsp. pepper

2 cloves garlic, minced

1 lb. cooked chicken, shredded OR 15 oz. canned chunk chicken in water, drained

12 corn tortillas

Cooking spray

1 c. part–skim mozzarella cheese, shredded

Yield:
12 enchiladas
6 servings

Serving Size:
2 enchiladas

Preparation Time:
25 minutes

Cooking Time:
20 minutes

Nutrient Analysis per serving:

Calories: 384
Fat: 13.6 gm
Cholesterol: 75 mg
Sodium: 610 mg

Preheat oven to 375°. Combine onion, green pepper, green chilies, chicken broth and ⅓ cup of enchilada sauce in a large, nonstick skillet; cook for 5 minutes. Add chili powder, pepper, garlic and chicken. Mix well, cover and simmer for 5 minutes or until thoroughly heated. Meanwhile, heat corn tortillas by wrapping them in paper towels and microwaving at HIGH for 1-½ to 2 minutes. Spread ⅓ cup of chicken mixture lengthwise on each tortilla. Roll tortilla and place, seam side down, in a shallow baking dish coated with cooking spray; pour remaining enchilada sauce over and sprinkle with cheese. Bake for 20 minutes or until thoroughly heated.

Mexican Beef Stir–Fry

Quick and easy stir–frying techniques are used for this south–of–the–border meal.

Yield:
4 servings

Serving Size:
1 ½ cup

Preparation Time:
20 minutes

Cooking Time:
8–10 minutes

Nutrient Analysis per serving:

Calories: 248
Fat: 11.8 gm
Cholesterol: 65 mg
Sodium: 68 mg

1 lb. lean beef top round steak

1 ½ T. oil

1 tsp. <u>each</u> cumin and dried whole oregano leaves

1 clove garlic, minced

1 green pepper, cut into thin strips

1 medium onion, cut into thin wedges

1–2 jalapeno peppers, seeded and cut into slivers

1 tomato, chopped

3 c. romaine lettuce, cut into ¼-inch slices

¼ c. sharp reduced–fat Cheddar cheese, shredded

4 flour tortillas

Cut beef into thin strips. Combine oil, cumin, oregano and garlic. Heat half the seasoned oil mixture in a large wok over medium–high heat until hot. Stir–fry beef strips (half at a time) until done; remove from wok and set aside. In remaining oil mixture, stir–fry green pepper, onion and jalapeno peppers for 1–2 minutes. Add tomato and continue to stir–fry 1 more minute. Return meat to wok with vegetables and heat thoroughly. Spoon beef mixture over lettuce, sprinkle with cheese and serve with warm tortillas.

The wok is the favored cooking utensil for stir–frying because its sloped sides allow an even distribution of heat and quick cooking. However, a large skillet or an electric skillet also work well.

214

Pronto Taco Bake

1 lb. lean ground beef
1 pkg. (1 $\frac{1}{8}$ oz.) taco seasoning
$\frac{1}{2}$ c. water
1 can (12 oz.) whole kernel corn, drained
$\frac{1}{2}$ c. green pepper, chopped
1 can (8 oz.) tomato sauce
Cooking spray
1 pkg. (8 $\frac{1}{2}$ oz.) corn muffin mix
$\frac{1}{2}$ c. green onions, sliced and divided
$\frac{1}{3}$ c. part–skim mozzarella cheese, shredded

Yield:
  6 servings
Serving Size:
  4x3$\frac{3}{4}$-inch piece
Preparation Time:
  15 minutes
Cooking Time:
  25 minutes

Preheat oven to 400°. In skillet, brown meat; drain. Stir in taco seasoning, water, corn, green pepper and tomato sauce. Pour into a 12x7$\frac{1}{2}$x2-inch baking dish coated with cooking spray. In a separate bowl, prepare corn muffin mix according to package directions; add $\frac{1}{4}$ cup green onions. Spoon muffin mixture around outer edge of casserole. Bake uncovered for 20 minutes. Top cornbread with cheese and remaining onions; bake 2–3 minutes longer.

Hint: You can lower the sodium content of this dish by deleting the taco seasoning and using chili powder and garlic powder.

*Nutrient Analysis
per serving:*

Calories: 440
Fat: 17.7 gm
Cholesterol: 65 mg
Sodium: 1,110 mg

Firecracker Enchilada Casserole

Yield:
8 servings

Serving Size:
4 ½ x 3 ¼-inch piece

Preparation Time:
25 minutes

Cooking Time:
25 minutes

1 lb. ground turkey
1 medium onion, chopped
2 cans (8 oz. each) tomato sauce
1 can (12 oz.) mexicorn, drained
1 can (10 oz.) mild enchilada sauce
½ tsp. chili powder
¼ tsp. dried whole oregano
12 corn tortillas
1 ½ c. part–skim mozzarella cheese, shredded
1 c. lettuce, shredded
½ c. tomatoes, chopped

Nutrient Analysis per serving:

Calories: 334
Fat: 12 gm
Cholesterol: 49 mg
Sodium: 876 mg

Preheat oven to 350°. Cook turkey and onion in a large nonstick skillet until browned; drain fat. Add tomato sauce, mexicorn, enchilada sauce and seasonings; mix well. Bring to a boil; reduce heat and simmer for 5 minutes. Place 6 tortillas in the bottom of a 13x9x2-inch baking dish. Pour half of meat mixture over tortillas; sprinkle with one–half of mozzarella cheese. Repeat layers of tortillas and meat. Bake for 20 minutes. Sprinkle with remaining mozzarella cheese and bake an additional 5 minutes. Garnish with lettuce and tomato. (If prepared ahead of time, refrigerate covered. Allow 40 minutes heating time; sprinkle with mozzarella cheese 5 minutes before serving.)

Look closely at the label on a package of corn tortillas and you'll find a simple list of ingredients: ground corn, water, a trace of lime. Corn tortillas contain no fat. Flour tortillas, however, list lard as an ingredient.

Carne Adovado

Spicy traditional dish for those who like it <u>hot</u>.

1/4 c. hot chili powder
1/4 c. mild chil powder
2 cloves garlic, minced
1 T. cumin
1 T. dried whole oregano
1/2 tsp. salt
1 1/2 c. water
3 lb. lean center–cut pork chops,
    trimmed of visible fat

Combine all ingredients except pork. Place pork chops in a 12x7^1/$_2$x2-inch baking dish. Pour chili mixture over chops and bake at 325° for 45 minutes. Uncover and continue to bake 30 more minutes. Let cool and shred pork. Serve with flour tortillas, lettuce and plain nonfat yogurt.

Yield:
    8 servings
Serving Size:
    5 ounces
Preparation Time:
    10 minutes
Cooking Time:
    1 ^{1}/$_4$ hours

**Nutrient Analysis
per serving:**

Calories: 248
Fat: 13 gm
Cholesterol: 80 mg
Sodium: 291 mg

Recipes containing chili powder may not need much salt since salt is one of the ingredient in most commercial chili powders.

Mock Sangria

Tastes better than the real thing.

Yield:
14 cups
28 servings

Serving Size:
½ cup

Preparation Time:
5–10 minutes

Nutrient Analysis per serving:

Calories: 47
Fat: 0 gm
Cholesterol: 0 mg
Sodium: 10 mg

1 bottle (40 oz.) unsweetened white grape juice, chilled
1 bottle (32 oz.) apple–cranberry juice, chilled
½ c. lime juice, chilled
1 bottle (33.8 oz.) club soda, chilled
GARNISH:
Seedless green grapes
Sliced limes
Sliced oranges

Combine juices. Just before serving, add club soda; stir and garnish.

VEGETARIAN ENTREES

VEGETARIAN ENTREES

Claim Jumper's Black Bean Stew

2 tsp. olive oil
1 large red onion, chopped
1 can (15 oz.) black beans, rinsed and drained
1 can (16 oz.) stewed tomatoes
3 T. dried parsley flakes
½ tsp. coriander
¼ tsp. garlic powder
4 c. cooked rice
1 ⅓ T. Parmesan cheese, grated

In a large nonstick skillet, heat oil; add and onion and sauté until onion is transparent. Add beans and remaining ingredients except rice and Parmesan cheese; bring to a boil. Reduce heat and simmer for 20 minutes to allow flavors to blend. Serve over hot rice and sprinkled with Parmesan cheese.

Yield:
4 servings

Serving Size:
1 ¾ cups

Preparation Time:
15 minutes

Cooking Time:
20 minutes

Nutrient Analysis per serving:

Calories:	419
Fat:	3.1 gm
Cholesterol:	1 mg
Sodium:	52 mg

For a meatless recipe to be classified as a main dish in Simply Colorado, it must contain at least 10 grams of protein per serving.

Confetti Couscous Casserole

1 ½ c. water

¼ tsp. salt

1 c. couscous

Cooking spray

¾ c. sweet red pepper, chopped

1/2 c. onion, chopped

1 clove garlic, minced

1 can (15 oz.) black beans, drained and rinsed

1 can (8¾ oz.) no–salt–added whole kernel corn, drained

1 can (8 oz.) sliced water chestnuts, drained

⅓ c. green onions, sliced

2 T. pickled or fresh jalapeno pepper, seeded and minced

1 c. lite ricotta cheese

2 T. white wine vinegar

2 tsp. sesame oil

1 tsp. cumin

½ c. (4 oz.) reduced–fat sharp Cheddar cheese, shredded

Yield:
4 servings

Serving Size:
1½ cups

Preparation Time:
20 minutes

Cooking Time:
25 minutes

Nutrient Analysis per serving:

Calories: 583
Fat: 11.9 gm
Cholesterol: 19 mg
Sodium: 956 mg

Preheat oven to 350°. Combine water and salt in a large saucepan; bring to a boil. Remove from heat and stir in couscous. Cover and let stand 5 minutes or until couscous is tender and liquid is absorbed. Coat a nonstick skillet with cooking spray; add red pepper, onion and garlic. Saute' until tender. Add pepper mixture, black beans, corn, water chestnuts, green onions and jalapeno pepper to couscous; stir gently. Combine ricotta cheese, vinegar, sesame oil and cumin; stir into couscous mixture. Spoon mixture into a 12x7x2-inch glass casserole dish coated with cooking spray. Cover and bake 20 minutes. Uncover, sprinkle with cheese and return to oven for 5 minutes more or until cheese melts and dish is thoroughly heated.

Couscous is a Middle Eastern grain made from precooked semolina wheat. It is usually served with spicy meat and vegetable dishes.

LaJunta Lentil Bake

A hearty dish with a delicate herb flavor.

¾ c. dry lentils
½ c. onion, chopped
2 tsp. dried whole basil leaves
1 tsp. oil
1 c. (4 oz.) part–skim mozzarella cheese, shredded
1 can (16. oz.) canned diced tomatoes, drained and divided
2 eggs (or ½ c. egg substitute)
½ tsp. dried whole oregano
½ tsp. salt
Cooking spray

Yield:
   4 servings
Serving Size:
   1 ½ cups
Preparation Time:
   15 minutes
Cooking Time:
   45 minutes for
     lentils plus
   50 minutes baking

Cook lentils according to package directions. In a nonstick skillet, sauté onion and basil in oil until transparent. Combine lentils, onion mixture, cheese, half of tomatoes, eggs, oregano and salt; pour into an 8x8-inch pan coated with cooking spray. Top with remaining tomatoes. Bake, uncovered, at 350° for 45–60 minutes or until set in center.

Nutrient Analysis per serving:

Calories:	252
Fat:	8 gm
Cholesterol:	107 mg
Sodium:	562 mg

Simmer dried beans over low heat, as a rolling boil may cause them to break or burst.

Mesa Verde Black Beans with Rice

Yield:
6 servings

Serving Size:
1 cup

Preparation Time:
15–20 minutes

Cooking Time:
30 minutes

Nutrient Analysis per serving:

Calories: 406
Fat: 1.3 gm
Cholesterol: 0 mg
Sodium: 333 mg

Cooking spray
1 c. onion, chopped
1 c. green pepper, chopped
4 cloves garlic, minced
2 cans (15 oz. each) black beans, drained
2 c. water
¼ tsp. crushed red pepper flakes
¼ tsp. salt
1 can (6 oz.) tomato paste
1 T. vinegar
4 ½ c. cooked long–grain rice
½ c. tomatoes, chopped
¼ c. green onions, sliced
¼ c. plain nonfat yogurt

Coat a large Dutch oven with cooking spray. Place over medium heat; add onion, green pepper and garlic; sauté until tender, stirring often. Add black beans, water, crushed red pepper flakes and salt. Bring to a boil; cover, reduce heat and simmer 15 minutes, stirring occasionally. Add tomato paste and vinegar; uncover and cook 15 minutes longer or until thickened (not too much liquid). Serve over ¾ cup rice and top evenly with chopped tomatoes, sliced green onion, and nonfat yogurt.

Acid in tomato products and vinegar tend to harden beans — that's why they're added last.

Spinach Enchilada Casserole

1 medium onion, chopped
Cooking spray
1 pkg. (10 oz.) frozen chopped spinach, thawed
2 cans (8 oz. each) tomato sauce
1 can (12 oz.) mexicorn, drained
1 can (10 oz.) mild enchilada sauce
1 tsp. chili powder
1/4 tsp. dried whole oregano
12 corn tortillas
6 oz. part–skim mozzarella cheese, shredded
1 c. lettuce, shredded
1/2 c. fresh tomatoes, chopped

Yield:
  8 servings
Serving Size:
  4 1/2x3 1/4-inch
  piece
Preparation Time:
  25 minutes
Cooking Time:
  25minutes

Preheat oven to 350°. Sauté onion in a large, nonstick skillet coated with cooking spray. Drain spinach and pat out excess moisture between 2 paper towels. Combine onion, spinach, tomato sauce, mexicorn, enchilada sauce and seasonings; mix well. Bring to a boil; reduce heat and simmer for 5 minutes. Place 6 tortillas in the bottom of a 13x9x2-inch baking dish. Pour half of spinach mixture over tortillas; sprinkle with one–half of mozzarella cheese. Repeat layers of tortillas and spinach mixture. Bake for 20 minutes. Sprinkle with remaining mozzarella cheese and bake an additional 5 minutes. Garnish with lettuce and tomato. (If prepared ahead of time, refrigerate covered. Allow 40 minutes heating time; sprinkle with mozzarella cheese 5 minutes before serving.)

*Nutrient Analysis
per serving:*

Calories: 260
Fat: 8 gm
Cholesterol: 12 mg
Sodium: 503 mg

Look closely at the label on a package of corn tortillas and you'll find a simple list of ingredients: ground corn, water, a trace of lime. Corn tortillas contain no fat. Flour tortillas, however, list lard as an ingredient.

225

Lean and Luscious Potato Split

Bake extra potatoes to have ready for this scrumptious entree.

Yield:
2 servings

Serving Size:
$^1/_2$ potato

Preparation Time:
20 minutes

Cooking Time:
10–12 minutes

Nutrient Analysis per serving:

Calories: 163
Fat: 4.1 gm
Cholesterol: 2 mg
Sodium: 587 mg

1 large potato, baked
3 T. skim milk
$^1/_4$ c. 1% cottage cheese
2 T. <u>each</u> chopped green pepper, chopped carrot and sliced green onions
1 T. sunflower seeds
$^1/_4$ c. sharp reduced–fat Cheddar cheese, shredded
$^1/_8$ tsp. garlic salt
$^1/_8$ tsp. pepper
3 cherry tomatoes, halved

Preheat oven to 450°. Halve and scoop out potato pulp, leaving $^1/_4$ inch in shells. Mash potato pulp in bowl. Add milk, cottage cheese, green pepper, carrot, onion, sunflower seeds, half the Cheddar cheese, salt and pepper. Gently mix to blend thoroughly. Mound into potato shells, dividing equally. Arrange 3 tomato halves on each potato half, pushing in slightly. Sprinkle with remaining Cheddar cheese. Bake for 10–12 minutes or until cheese is melted and potatoes are heated thoroughly.

Hint: Potatoes may be prepared in advance up to the point of heating. Wrap them securely and refrigerate up to 2 days. Reheat in conventional oven or microwave.

Bluish–gray discoloration sometimes found after cooking potatoes results from substances reacting with the iron in the potato. Greening in potatoes, however, may indicate the presence of solanine, a toxin that could be hazardous only in large amounts.

226

Vegetable Calzones

1 loaf (1 lb.) frozen bread dough
Cooking spray
1 c. fresh mushrooms, sliced
3/4 c. sweet red pepper, chopped
1/2 c. onion, chopped
1 pkg. (10 oz.) frozen chopped spinach, thawed
1 c. lite ricotta cheese
1/4 c. Parmesan cheese, grated
1/2 c. (2 oz.) part–skim mozzarella cheese,
  shredded
1/2 tsp. Italian seasoning
2 c. commercial low–fat spaghetti sauce

Yield:
  4 servings
Serving Size:
  1 calzone
Preparation Time:
  30 minutes
Cooking Time:
  15–20 minutes

*Nutrient Analysis
per serving:*

Calories: 542
Fat: 14 gm
Cholesterol: 34 mg
Sodium: 858 mg

Let bread rise according to package directions. Preheat oven to 400°. Coat a nonstick skillet with cooking spray; place over medium heat and add mushrooms, red pepper and onion. Sauté until tender; remove from heat. Drain spinach and squeeze out excess moisture. Combine spinach, cheeses and Italian seasoning; mix well. Add sautéed vegetables and mix well. Punch bread dough down and divide into 4 equal portions. Shape each portion into an 8-inch circle. Spoon 2/3 cup vegetable/cheese mixture onto 1/2 of each circle, leaving a 1/2-inch border. Moisten edges of circle with water. Fold plain half of each circle over filling, crimping edges to seal. Place calzones on baking sheet coated with cooking spray. Bake 15–20 minutes or until golden brown. Serve with 1/2 cup spaghetti sauce.

Manicotti in Minutes

Unbelievably simple!

Yield:
7 servings

Serving Size:
2 manicotti

Preparation Time:
20 minutes

Cooking Time:
50 minutes

Nutrient Analysis per serving:

Calories: 404
Fat: 11.4 gm
Cholesterol: 15 mg
Sodium: 789 mg

1 jar (26 oz.) commercial low–fat spaghetti sauce
1 can (16 oz.) diced tomatoes
1 clove garlic, minced
2 c. 1% cottage cheese
1 c. lite ricotta cheese
3 T. Parmesan cheese
2 egg whites
4 T. fresh parsley, chopped
8 oz. manicotti shells (14 shells), uncooked
1 c. water

Preheat oven to 450°. Combine spaghetti sauce, tomatoes and garlic; set aside. Combine cheeses, egg whites and parsley; stuff manicotti shells with cheese mixture using a small spatula. Fill bottom of a 12x7x2-inch casserole dish with 2 cups tomato mixture. Arrange stuffed shells in a single layer over the sauce. Cover shells with remaining 3 cups sauce; pour water evenly over sauce. (Don't be concerned about the watery appearance, it will be absorbed during the cooking process.) Cover dish with foil and bake for 50 minutes. Remove foil and bake another 10 minutes.

Hint: This quick dish freezes well and can be warmed in the microwave.

Tomatoes canned without salt are allowed to ripen on the vine longer than those canned with salt so they will have more natural flavor.

Eggplant Parmesan

2–3 T. flour

1 lb. eggplant

2 egg whites

2 T. skim milk

²/₃ c. Italian breadcrumbs

Cooking spray

1 jar (26 oz.) commercial low–fat
    spaghetti sauce

1 ½ c. (6 oz.) part–skim mozzarella
    cheese shredded

3 T. Parmesan cheese, grated

Yield:
  6 servings

Serving Size:
  4½ x 4⅓-inch
    piece

Preparation Time:
  15–20 minutes

Cooking Time:
  30 minutes

Preheat oven to 400°. Place flour in a large zip–top plastic bag; set aside. Peel and cut eggplant into 12 half–inch thick slices. Place slices in plastic bag; shake to coat. Combine egg whites and milk. Dip each eggplant slice into egg white mixture and dredge lightly in Italian bread-crumbs. Place slices on a baking sheet coated with cooking spray. Bake 12–15 minutes or until lightly browned and tender. Reduce oven temperature to 350°. Coat a 13x9x2-inch baking dish with cooking spray. Place half the eggplant slices in a single layer on the bottom of the dish. Spoon half the spaghetti sauce over the slices and sprinkle with half the mozzarella cheese. Repeat a second layer with the remaining ingre-dients. Top with Parmesan cheese and bake uncovered 15 minutes, or until thoroughly heated.

*Nutrient Analysis
per serving:*

Calories: 314
Fat: 12.3 gm
Cholesterol: 19 mg
Sodium: 680 mg

Choose eggplant that has uniform thickness so servings will be equal. Fresh eggplant should be glossy with a fresh–looking cap.

Lentil Spaghetti Sauce

Yield:
   5 servings
Serving Size:
   1 cup
Preparation Time:
   20 minutes
Cooking Time:
   1 hour, 15 minutes

Nutrient Analysis per serving:

Calories: 287
Fat: 2.3 gm
Cholesterol: 0 mg
Sodium: 518 mg

Cooking spray
³/₄ c. onion, chopped
¹/₂ c. green pepper, chopped
3 cloves garlic, minced
2 cans (14¹/₂ oz. each) low–sodium
   chicken broth
1 ¹/₂ c. dried lentils, uncooked
1 tsp. crushed red pepper flakes
¹/₂ tsp. salt
1 can (16 oz.) diced tomatoes
1 can (6 oz.) tomato paste
1 T. vinegar
1 tsp. Italian seasoning

Coat a Dutch oven with cooking spray. Add onion, pepper and garlic; sauté over medium heat until tender. Add broth, lentils, red pepper and salt. Bring to a boil; cover, reduce heat and simmer 30 minutes. Stir in tomatoes, tomato paste, vinegar and Italian seasoning. Bring to a boil; reduce heat and simmer 45 minutes or until desired consistency, stirring often. Serve over hot cooked spaghetti noodles.

Cast iron pots and skillets are good sources of iron, especially when cooking acidic foods such as spaghetti sauce.

KIDS CUISINE

KIDS CUISINE

Cinnamon and Sugar Wonton Chips

Make a batch before your next long–distance car trip. They're great to snack on!

20 (4-inch square each) wonton skins
Water
1 tsp. cinnamon
¼ c. sugar

Preheat oven to 350°. Cut wonton skins in quarters by making 2 diagonal cuts forming an "X". Arrange wonton skins in a single layer on ungreased baking sheet; spray lightly with water. Combine cinnamon and sugar; sprinkle evenly over wet wonton skins. Bake for 5 minutes or until lightly brown. Let cool on baking sheet then remove. Store in airtight container.

Yield:
  80 wedges
  20 servings

Serving Size:
  4 wedges

Preparation Time:
  5 minutes

Cooking Time:
  5 minutes

Nutrient Analysis per serving:

Calories: 33
Fat: .4 gm
Cholesterol: 0 mg
Sodium: 0 mg

You can find wonton skins in the produce section of your local supermarket.

Mini Muffin Pizzas

*One of your child's favorite foods
to make at home.*

Yield:
  8 pizzas

Serving Size:
  1 pizza

Preparation Time:
  5 minutes

Cooking Time:
  10 minutes

**Nutrient Analysis
per serving:**

Calories: 184
Fat: 7 gm
Cholesterol: 18 mg
Sodium: 499 mg

4 English muffins, split
1 can (8 oz.) pizza sauce
1 cup part–skim mozzarella cheese, shredded
Assorted pizza toppings (optional)

Lightly toast muffins. Spread one generous tablespoon of pizza sauce on each muffin half. Sprinkle with cheese; top with your favorite pizza topping (green pepper, mushrooms, pepperoni, etc.). Bake muffin pizza in a 400° oven until cheese melts (about 6 minutes).

*Provide a wide variety
of nutrient–rich foods.
Then trust your child's
instincts about the
amount they will eat.*

Chicken Nuggets

Your children will enjoy helping you prepare this casual entree.

1 egg

2 T. milk

3 c. cornflakes, finely crushed

1 lb. boneless chicken breast, cut into
    1 or 1½-inch bite–sized pieces

Cooking spray

Preheat oven to 400°. Whisk eggs and milk together in a small bowl; set aside. Place cornflake crumbs in a gallon–sized zip–top bag. Dip each chicken piece in the egg/milk mixture, then let the kids help by shaking the pieces in the cornflake crumb bag. Place each coated nugget on a cookie sheet coated with cooking spray. Bake for 15 minutes or until done. Serve with your favorite dipping sauce.

Yield:
    6 servings

Serving Size:
    about 6 nuggets

Preparation Time:
    10–15 minutes

Cooking Time:
    15 minutes

Nutrient Analysis per serving:

Calories: 148
Fat: 2.6 gm
Cholesterol: 78 mg
Sodium: 170 mg

Invite your child to help with meal preparation. They can do anything from tearing lettuce to setting the table.

Sloppy Toms

A healthy version of an old favorite.

Yield:
4 servings

Serving Size:
1 sandwich

Preparation Time:
5 minutes

Cooking Time:
15–20 minutes

Nutrient Analysis per serving:

Calories: 335
Fat: 6 gm
Cholesterol: 66 mg
Sodium: 708 mg

Cooking spray
1 lb. ground turkey
³/₄ c. onion, chopped
¹/₂ c. green pepper, chopped
2 cloves garlic, minced
1 can (8 oz.) tomato sauce
¹/₄ c. catsup
1 tsp. chili powder
Salt and pepper to taste
4 whole wheat hamburger buns

Coat a large nonstick skillet with cooking spray; place skillet over medium–high heat. Add ground turkey, onion, green pepper and garlic; cook until browned, stirring to crumble turkey. Drain well. To turkey mixture, add tomato sauce, catsup, chili powder, salt and pepper. Cook over medium heat 10 minutes, stirring occasionally. Divide mixture evenly among hamburger buns.

Don't worry about how much your child eats at a single meal. Over a week, their choices usually even out and provide a balance that meets their needs.

Peanut Butter Bread

With a glass of milk this makes a popular after–school snack.

½ c. chunky peanut butter
⅓ c. nonfat dry milk
1 egg
¼ c. honey
1 c. water
2 c. flour
2 tsp. baking powder
¼ tsp. baking soda
Cooking spray

Preheat oven to 350°. In a medium–size bowl, blend peanut butter, milk, egg, honey and water. In a separate bowl, mix together flour, baking powder and baking soda. Add the flour mixture to the peanut butter mixture; stirring just until dry ingredients are moistened — **do not over-mix**. Spoon into a 9x5-inch loaf pan coated with cooking spray. Bake for 35–40 minutes. Cool on a wire rack for 15 minutes. Remove loaf from pan and cool completely before serving.

Yield:
 1 loaf
 20 slices
Serving Size:
 1 slice
Preparation Time:
 15 minutes
Cooking Time:
 35–40 minutes

Nutrient Analysis per serving:

Calories: 101
Fat: 3.5 gm
Cholesterol: 9 mg
Sodium: 118 mg

Try not to use food as a reward. If you do, your child will look for food as a source of love and comfort — and ignore her internal mechanism that signals when to eat.

Pumpkin–Oat Pancakes

This pancake is a Halloween favorite given to us by Wildwood Resources and Child Care Food Program

Yield:
   8 pancakes
   4 servings

Serving Size:
   2 pancakes

Preparation Time:
   10 minutes

Cooking Time:
   5–10 minutes

Nutrient Analysis per serving:

Calories: 238
Fat: 6.3 gm
Cholesterol: 48 mg
Sodium: 377 mg

For a special Halloween treat, make a jack–o–lantern face. On a medium–hot griddle or nonstick skillet, drop 2 tsp. batter in circles for eyes and spoon batter in a semi–circle for the mouth. Cook until light brown and then pour about 1/3 cup batter over the eyes and mouth. Cook pancake until light brown and bubbly, then turn pancake.

1 c. low–fat buttermilk

$\frac{1}{2}$ c. regular oats, uncooked

$\frac{1}{2}$ c. skim milk

$\frac{1}{2}$ c. pumpkin, mashed and cooked

1 egg

1 egg white

1 T. oil

$\frac{1}{3}$ c. flour

$\frac{1}{3}$ c. whole wheat flour

2 T. sugar

2 T. wheat germ

1 tsp. baking powder

$\frac{1}{2}$ tsp. baking soda

$\frac{1}{4}$ tsp. cinnamon

Cooking spray

Combine buttermilk and oats; let mixture stand for 15 minutes. Add milk, pumpkin, egg, egg white and oil to oat mixture; mix well. In a small bowl, combine the remaining ingredients; stir into pumpkin mixture until batter is smooth. Coat a hot griddle with cooking spray. Pour about $\frac{1}{4}$ cup of batter onto griddle. Cook until bubbles start to burst on first side; flip pancake and cook on other side.

Waffle Sundae

A clever breakfast that's fun to eat.

2 toaster waffles
1 can (8 oz.) crushed pineapple, reserve juice
1 carton (8 oz.) vanilla low-fat yogurt

Toast waffles according to package directions. Evenly spread pineapple onto each waffle. Mix 3 tablespoons of pineapple juice with yogurt and spoon onto fruit–topped waffle.

Berry Breakfast Shake

Not enough time for breakfast? This shake can accompany you on your drive to work.

1 c. cold skim milk
1 banana, frozen (or fresh banana and ¹/₂ c. ice)
¹/₄ c. frozen raspberries or other frozen berries

Combine all ingredients in blender and process until smooth.

Hint: Freeze bananas without peels and they will be much easier to use.

Yield:
2 servings

Serving Size:
1 waffle

Preparation Time:
5 minutes

Cooking Time:
3 minutes

Nutrient Analysis per serving:

Calories: 354
Fat: 6.1 gm
Cholesterol: 99 mg
Sodium: 558 mg

Yield:
1 serving

Serving Size:
1 ¹/₂ cups

Preparation Time:
3–5 minutes

Nutrient Analysis per serving:

Calories: 206
Fat: 1.2 gm
Cholesterol: 4 mg
Sodium: 128 mg

The average American doesn't get enough calcium. Make sure that every day you consume calcium– rich foods such as low–fat dairy products and green leafy vegetables.

239

Crunchy Bananas

2 bananas
$^1/_2$ c. orange juice
$^1/_3$ c. coconut, granola or chopped nuts

Yield:
4 servings

Serving Size:
$^1/_2$ banana

Preparation Time:
5 minutes

Peel bananas and cut into one-inch thick slices. Dip each slice in orange juice then roll in the crunchy topping. Serve as a fun fingerfood snack or freeze to make a warm weather treat.

Nutrient Analysis per serving:

Calories: 83
Fat: 2 gm
Cholesterol: 0 mg
Sodium: 31 mg

Crowded Canoes

Yield:
8 pieces

Serving Size:
1 canoe

Preparation Time:
5 minutes

4 celery stalks
$^1/_2$ c. creamy peanut butter or spreadable cheese
$^1/_4$ c. raisins

Clean celery and cut each stalk into 2 4-inch pieces. Spread one tablespoon of peanut butter or cheese in the curves of the celery. Decorate with raisins.

Nutrient Analysis per serving:

Calories: 110
Fat: 7 gm
Cholesterol: 0 mg
Sodium: 94 mg

Orange Smoothie

1 can (6 oz.) frozen orange juice concentrate
1 c. low-fat milk
1/2 c. cold water
1/2 tsp. vanilla
10 ice cubes

Place all ingredients in a blender. Process until frothy and smooth. Serve immediately.

Yield:
  4 servings
Serving Size:
  2/3 cup
Preparation Time:
  3 minutes

Nutrient Analysis per serving:

Calories: 100
Fat: 1.2 gm
Cholesterol: 4 mg
Sodium: 36 mg

Honey Hug

The perfect drink after a day of sledding.

2 c. low-fat milk
2 tsp. honey
1 tsp. vanilla
Cinnamon

Heat milk over low heat, stir in honey and vanilla. To serve, pour into two mugs and garnish with cinnamon.

Yield:
  2 servings
Serving Size:
  1 cup
Preparation Time:
  1 minutes
Cooking Time:
  3 minutes

Nutrient Analysis per serving:

Calories: 114
Fat: .4 gm
Cholesterol: 4 mg
Sodium: 127 mg

Make eating a positive experience — a time for fun and enjoyment.

Peanutty Chocolate Pops

Cool and refreshing!

Yield:
4 servings

Serving Size:
1 pop

Preparation Time:
5 minutes

Freezing Time:
4 or more hours

Nutrient Analysis per serving:

Calories: 271
Fat: 15 gm
Cholesterol: 5 mg
Sodium: 209 mg

³/₄ c. low-fat milk
¹/₂ c. creamy peanut butter
¹/₄ c. nonfat dry milk
¹/₄ c. plain low-fat yogurt
2 T. honey
1 tsp. unsweetened cocoa powder

Combine all ingredients in a blender. Process until smooth. Pour mixture into four 5-ounce paper cups. Cover cups with foil; insert wooden sticks through foil into mixture. Freeze several hours until firm. To serve, remove foil and tear off paper cup.

Increase the calcium in your child's diet by fortifying recipes with nonfat dry milk powder.

DESSERTS

Redstone Rhubarb Crisp

6 c. fresh or frozen rhubarb, diced
Cooking spray
$^{1}/_{2}$ c. brown sugar, packed
$^{1}/_{3}$ c. flour
$^{1}/_{3}$ c. regular oats, uncooked
$^{1}/_{2}$ tsp. cinnamon
2 T. margarine

Yield:
  6 servings
Serving Size:
  $^{1}/_{2}$ cup
Preparation Time:
  15 minutes
Cooking Time:
  30 minutes

Preheat oven to 350°. Place rhubarb in an 8-inch square baking pan coated with cooking spray. In a small bowl combine brown sugar, flour, oats and cinnamon. Cut in margarine until consistency of coarse meal. Sprinkle mixture over rhubarb, then bake for 30 minutes or until topping is lightly browned.

Nutrient Analysis per serving:

Calories: 255
Fat: 6.7 gm
Cholesterol: 0 mg
Sodium: 84 mg

245

Bananas Grand Marnier

*This special dessert is irresistible —
but don't eat all four servings yourself!*

Yield:
　4 servings

Serving Size:
　½ cup

Preparation Time:
　5 minutes

Cooking Time:
　3–5 minutes

**Nutrient Analysis
per serving:**

Calories:　　　144
Fat:　　　　　3.3 gm
Cholesterol:　0 mg
Sodium:　　　35 mg

1 T. margarine
⅓ c. orange juice
½ T. honey
2 T. *Grand Marnier* or orange–flavored liqueur
¼ tsp. vanilla
3 bananas, sliced
Ground cinnamon

Melt margarine in a saucepan; stir in orange juice, honey, *Grand Marnier* and vanilla. Add banana and simmer about 3 minutes or until thoroughly heated, stirring frequently. Serve warm, garnished with cinnamon.

NOTE: Also good served over frozen vanilla low–fat yogurt.

Bananas that are beginning to turn brown should be stored in the refrigerator to slow down ripening. The skin will turn black but the fruit will not be over–ripe.

Western Slope Peach Melba

1 pkg. (12 oz.) frozen raspberries
2 T. low–sugar raspberry jelly or spread
2 peaches, sliced
2 c. vanilla nonfat frozen yogurt

Yield:
  4 servings

Serving Size:
  1 cup

Preparation Time:
  5 minutes

Cooking Time:
  3 minutes

Combine raspberries and jelly in a glass bowl. Microwave on MEDIUM for 2–3 minutes or until raspberries are slightly warm; stir to mix in jelly. Divide peaches evenly into 4 bowls, top with a $1/2$ cup scoop of yogurt. Pour raspberry sauce evenly over 4 portions and serve.

Nutrient Analysis per serving:

Calories: 153
Fat: 1.2 gm
Cholesterol: 0 mg
Sodium: 11 mg

Chocolate Meringue Kisses

Served with fresh fruit, these light, sweet cookies are guilt–free (only 12 calories a piece!).

Yield:
40 cookies

Serving Size:
1 cookie

Preparation Time:
20 minutes

Cooking Time:
50–60 minutes

Nutrient Analysis per serving:

Calories: 12
Fat: 0 gm
Cholesterol: 0 mg
Sodium: 5 mg

3 egg whites, at room temperature
¼ tsp. cream of tartar
½ c. sugar
3 T. cocoa powder
1 tsp. vanilla

Preheat oven to 200°. Line two baking sheets with aluminum foil; set aside. In a small bowl, beat egg whites and cream of tartar at HIGH speed of an electric mixer until soft peaks form. Gradually add sugar 2 tablespoons at a time, beating after each addition until sugar is dissolved. Add cocoa powder and vanilla; continue beating until stiff, glossy peaks form. Spoon meringue by the tablespoonful onto baking sheets forming chocolate kiss shapes. Bake 1 hour or until set. Let cool on cookie sheets for 10 minutes. Carefully loosen and remove cookies with spatula and completely cool them on wire racks. Store in an airtight container.

Cocoa is much lower in fat than baking chocolate, and it doesn't have the high saturated fat content.

Fruit Custard Dessert Pizza

CRUST:

1/2 c. 1% small curd cottage cheese

3 T. margarine, softened

1 T. plain nonfat yogurt

1 c. flour

1/2 c. regular oats, uncooked

1 tsp. grated lemon peel

1/4 tsp. salt

Cooking spray

TOPPING:

1/2 c. low–sugar orange marmalade

1 pkg. (1.9 oz.) instant vanilla pudding

2 c. skim milk

1 orange, peeled and sliced in half moons

3 kiwis, peeled and sliced

1 pint strawberries, stemmed and cut in half

1 banana, peeled and sliced

1/4 fresh pineapple, peeled and in chunks

Yield:
8 servings

Serving Size:
1 wedge

Preparation Time:
25 minutes

Cooking Time:
15–20 minutes

Nutrient Analysis per serving:

Calories:	289
Fat:	5.7 gm
Cholesterol:	1 mg
Sodium:	255 mg

In small mixing bowl, combine cottage cheese, margarine and yogurt. Beat until smooth and well blended. In a large bowl combine flour, oats, lemon peel and salt. Stir cottage cheese mixture into flour mixture; stir well but do not overmix. Form into ball. With hands, press evenly into 12" pizza pan coated with cooking spray. Form a rim about 1/2" above the edge and crimp. Bake crust at 400° for 15–20 minutes. Cool thoroughly.

Topping: Heat marmalade until melted; set aside to cool slightly. Prepare pudding according to package directions using the 2 cups skim milk. Spread pudding into cooled crust. Arrange fruit atop pudding in this order: strawberries, pineapple, kiwi, oranges, banana. Drizzle fruit with melted marmalade. Cover with plastic wrap and chill.

249

Cherries in the Snow

Yield:
  10 servings

Serving Size:
  ¹/₁₀ of pie

Preparation Time:
  5 minutes
    (1 day ahead)
  20 minutes

Cooking Time:
  8–10 minutes

Chilling Time:
  2 hours

Nutrient Analysis per serving:

Calories: 350
Fat: 10.8 gm
Cholesterol: 21 mg
Sodium: 255 mg

1 carton (32 oz.) vanilla flavored low–fat yogurt
1 c. graham cracker crumbs
3 T. margarine, melted
¼ c. sugar
1 envelope unflavored gelatin
⅓ c. lemon juice
¾ c. sugar
1 tub (8 oz.) light cream cheese
2 tsp. grated lemon peel
1 can (21 oz.) cherry pie filling

Place colander in a large bowl; line colander with 2 coffee filters. Make yogurt cheese by spooning yogurt into colander. Cover loosely with plastic wrap; chill 24 hours. Discard liquid. Preheat oven to 350°. Combine graham cracker crumbs, margarine and sugar; mix well and press into a 9-inch pie plate. Bake for 8–10 minutes. Cool completely. In a small saucepan, sprinkle gelatin over lemon juice; let stand 1 minute. Add remaining sugar and cook over low heat, stirring until gelatin and sugar dissolve. Remove from heat; place in a blender. Add cream cheese, lemon peel and chilled yogurt cheese; blend until smooth. Pour into crust; cover and chill for 4 hours. Spoon cherry pie filling over top and serve.

Yogurt cheese is great on bagels or bread. It will keep in the refrigerator up to one week.

Fruit Burritos with Chocolate Sauce

2 c. fresh berries (strawberries or raspberries), cleaned and sliced
8 oz. vanilla flavored nonfat yogurt
4 small flour tortillas or prepared crepes
⅓ c. chocolate syrup
Fresh berries

In a small bowl, combine berries and yogurt; mix well. Place ¼ of the mixture on each tortilla and roll up. Place each burrito, seam side down, on a small plate and spoon chocolate syrup evenly over each burrito. Garnish with a few fresh berries.

Yield:
4 servings

Serving Size:
1 burrito

Preparation Time:
5–7 minutes

Nutrient Analysis per serving:

Calories: 163
Fat: 3.4 gm
Cholesterol: 0 mg
Sodium: 43 mg

Did you know that Hershey's Chocolate Syrup contains practically no fat?

Fresh Fruit Parfait

Transformed to elegance in a parfait glass.

Yield:
4 servings

Serving Size:
1 parfait

Preparation Time:
10–15 minutes

**Nutrient Analysis
per serving:**

Calories: 126
Fat: .6 gm
Cholesterol: 0 mg
Sodium: 32 mg

1 c. plain nonfat yogurt
2 T. maple syrup
1 tsp. vanilla
¹/₂ tsp. cinnamon
2 medium bananas, sliced
2 c. strawberries, sliced

Combine yogurt, syrup, vanilla and cinnamon. Layer bananas and strawberries in parfait glasses with sauce between each layer.

Easy Apple Extraordinaire

Yield:
1 serving

Serving Size:
1 apple

Preparation Time:
3 minutes

Cooking Time:
2 minutes

**Nutrient Analysis
per serving:**

Calories: 158
Fat: 5 gm
Cholesterol: 0 mg
Sodium: 2 mg

1 medium apple
¹/₈ tsp. cinnamon
1 T. raisins
1 T. nuts, chopped
¹/₃ c. nonfat vanilla frozen yogurt (optional)

Core apple and cut into bite–sized chunks; place in small microwaveable dish. Sprinkle with cinnamon; cover and microwave on HIGH for 1–2 minutes. Sprinkle with raisins and nuts, and serve. If desired, dollop with frozen yogurt.

Frozen Pumpkin Squares

2 c. cooked or canned pumpkin
$\frac{1}{2}$ c. sugar
1 tsp. ground ginger
$\frac{1}{2}$ tsp. nutmeg
$\frac{1}{2}$ gal. nonfat vanilla frozen yogurt
4 dozen gingersnaps

Combine pumpkin, sugar and spices; stir in yogurt. Line bottom of a 13x9x2-inch pan with gingersnaps. Pour half of pumpkin mixture over gingersnaps. Repeat layers and freeze. To serve, let set at room temperature for 5 minutes; cut into squares.

Yield:
18 servings
Serving Size:
3x2-inch piece
Preparation Time:
10–15 minutes
Freezing Time:
4–6 hours

Nutrient Analysis per serving:

Calories: 206
Fat: 2.6 gm
Cholesterol: 7 mg
Sodium: 107 mg

Make sure your frozen yogurt is made from skim or low–fat milk, those made from whole milk have considerably more fat.

253

Creative Carrot Cake

Moist and tasty — with or without frosting.

Yield:
 18 servings

Serving Size:
 3x2½-inch piece

Preparation Time:
 30 minutes

Cooking Time:
 40–45 minutes

Nutrient Analysis per serving:

Calories: 192
Fat: 6.1 gm
Cholesterol: 30 mg
Sodium: 220 mg

Cooking spray

1 c. boiling water

2 c. carrots, finely shredded

1 c. crushed pineapple with juice

⅔ c. shreds of wheat bran cereal (*All Bran*)

1 ¼ c. sugar

1 c. whole wheat flour

1 c. flour

3 eggs

½ c. raisins

½ c. walnuts, chopped

¼ c. oil

1 ¼ tsp. baking soda

1 tsp. vanilla

1 tsp. <u>each</u> cinnamon, nutmeg, ground
 cloves and salt

Preheat oven to 350°. Coat a 13x9x2-inch pan with cooking spray and dust with flour; set aside. Pour boiling water over carrots; set aside. In a large mixing bowl, combine crushed pineapple and cereal; let stand 5 minutes. Beat carrots and all remaining ingredients into cereal mixture at low speed of an electric mixer for 1 minute, scraping bowl constantly. Increase mixer speed to medium speed for 2 minutes. Pour batter into prepared pan. Bake for 40–45 minutes or until wooden pick inserted in center comes out clean. Serve with a sprinkle of powdered sugar.

Strawberry Lemon Trifle

*For the Fourth of July, make this with blueberries
and strawberries — a truly patriotic dessert.*

1 pkg. (3$^1/_2$ oz.) instant vanilla pudding
1 $^3/_4$ c. skim milk
12 oz. low–fat lemon flavored yogurt
1 angel food cake
1 qt. fresh strawberries, washed and sliced
$^1/_3$ c. sliced almonds, toasted

Yield:
  16 servings
Serving Size:
  1 cup
Preparation Time:
  15–20 minutes

Prepare vanilla pudding according to package
directions using 1$^3/_4$ cup skim milk. After
pudding has thickened, add yogurt and stir until
blended. Cut angel food cake into 1-inch cubes.
To assemble trifle, place $^1/_3$ of cake cubes on
bottom of a deep glass bowl; spread $^1/_3$ of
pudding mixture over cubes, then top with $^1/_3$ of
sliced strawberries. Repeat layers of cake,
pudding and strawberries 2 more times. Top with
sliced toasted almonds.

Hint: Use other fruit in season such as peaches,
raspberries and kiwi.

**Nutrient Analysis
per serving:**

Calories: 215
Fat: 2.1 gm
Cholesterol: 1 mg
Sodium: 131 mg

*To toast nuts, cover
bottom of microwave
with wax paper.
Spread with $^1/_4$ cup
chopped nuts.
Microwave uncover-
ed on HIGH for 5
minutes or until
lightly browned.*

New–Fashioned Oatmeal Cookies

Yield:
4 dozen

Serving Size:
1 cookie

Preparation Time:
20 minutes

Cooking Time:
9–10 minutes

Nutrient Analysis per serving:

Calories: 91
Fat: 3.8 gm
Cholesterol: 7 mg
Sodium: 45 mg

1 ¹/₂ c. flour
1 tsp. baking soda
¹/₂ tsp. salt
²/₃ c. oil
¹/₂ c. sugar
¹/₂ c. brown sugar, packed
2 eggs
1 tsp. vanilla
2 ¹/₂ c. regular oats, uncooked
1 c. raisins
¹/₃ c. sunflower seeds (optional)

Preheat oven to 375°. Combine flour, soda and salt; set side. In a large mixing bowl, beat together oil, sugars, eggs and vanilla at medium speed of an electric mixer. Slowly beat flour mixture into the oil mixture. Stir in oats, raisins and sunflower seeds. Drop by rounded tablespoonfuls onto an ungreased cookie sheet. Bake 9–10 minutes or until golden brown.

Peanutty Rice Krispie Pie

Kids love this dessert.

⅓ c. corn syrup
½ c. creamy peanut butter
2 c. *Rice Krispies*
1 qt. nonfat frozen yogurt of choice
Fresh fruit (optional)

Mix corn syrup, peanut butter and Rice Krispies together. Press into a 9-inch pie pan. Spoon frozen yogurt into *Rice Krispie* crust; freeze. If desired, top with fresh fruit or chocolate syrup before serving.

Yield:
10 servings

Serving Size:
¹/₁₀ of pie

Preparation Time:
10 minutes

Nutrient Analysis per serving:

Calories: 210
Fat: 6.8 gm
Cholesterol: 0 mg
Sodium: 77 mg

Frozen yogurt is a terrific dessert for ice cream lovers who want a lighter alternative. A half–cup serving of most frozen yogurts contains about 100 calories (17–20% of calories from fat). Regular and premium ice creams can range from 140 to 270 calories per half–cup serving (48–57% of calories from fat).

Cranberry Cottage Cake with Lemon Sauce

Looking for that extra–special dessert? You've found it!

Yield:
   12 servings

Serving Size:
   ¹/₁₂ of 9-inch cake
   with 2 T. sauce

Preparation Time:
   10–15 minutes

Cooking Time:
   40 minutes

Nutrient Analysis per serving:

Calories: 205
Fat: 5.9 gm
Cholesterol: 15 mg
Sodium: 147 mg

2 c. flour
²/₃ c. sugar
2 tsp. baking powder
²/₃ c. skim milk
1 egg, beaten
3 T. oil
½ tsp. lemon extract
2 c. whole cranberries, washed or
   2 c. fresh or frozen raspberries
Cooking spray

LEMON SAUCE:
¹/₃ c. sugar
1 T. cornstarch
1 c. boiling water
3 T. lemon juice
2 T. margarine
1 T. grated lemon peel

Preheat oven to 350°. Combine flour, sugar and baking powder in a mixing bowl. In a separate bowl stir together milk, egg, oil and extract. Pour milk mixture into flour mixture and stir until well blended. Stir in cranberries or raspberries (be careful not to crush raspberries). Pour into a 9-inch round cake pan coated with cooking spray. Bake for 40 minutes. Serve warm topped with lemon sauce.

Lemon Sauce: Combine sugar and cornstarch in a small saucepan. Add boiling water and cook over medium heat until thick and clear. Add lemon juice, margarine and rind. Stir until margarine melts. Serve warm over warm cake.

To get the most juice out of a lemon, lime or small orange, microwave fruit on HIGH for 30 to 45 seconds.

Fresh Apple Cake

*For those of you with an ample apple supply —
this is a delightfully delicious use of them!*

2 eggs, beaten
1 ¼ c. sugar
⅓ c. oil
4 c. apples (about 4–6 apples), grated
2 c. flour
2 tsp. cinnamon
1 tsp. baking soda
½ c. nuts, chopped
Cooking spray
2 T. powdered sugar

Yield:
  18 servings
Serving Size:
  3x2½-inch piece
Preparation Time:
  20 minutes
Cooking Time:
  40 minutes

**Nutrient Analysis
per serving:**

Calories:	183
Fat:	6.7 gm
Cholesterol:	20 mg
Sodium:	51 mg

Preheat oven to 350°. Stir eggs, sugar and oil together with a spoon. Stir in grated apple, flour, cinnamon and baking soda; mix well. Add chopped nuts. Pour into a 9x13-inch pan coated with cooking spray. Bake for 40 minutes. Let cool, then sprinkle with powdered sugar.

Orange Pound Cake

Unbelievably good — and so is the Chocolate Pound Cake variation.

Yield:
1 loaf
16 slices

Serving Size:
1 slice

Preparation Time:
15 minutes

Cooking Time:
45 minutes

Nutrient Analysis per serving:

Calories: 146
Fat: 7 gm
Cholesterol: 0 mg
Sodium: 96 mg

Cooking spray
1 ½ c. flour
¾ c. sugar
2 tsp. baking powder
½ c. oil
½ c. orange juice
1 tsp. grated orange peel
4 egg whites, stiffly beaten

Preheat oven to 350°. Coat the bottom of a 9 x 5-inch loaf pan with cooking spray; dust with flour and set aside. Combine flour, sugar and baking powder in large bowl; add oil and orange juice. Beat until well blended (batter will be thick). Add orange peel and about 1/3 of egg whites; stir gently. Fold in remaining egg whites. Spoon batter into prepared pan. Bake for 45 minutes or until done. Cool in pan for 10 minutes, then remove from pan and cool on wire rack.

Variation: For *Chocolate Pound Cake*, eliminate orange juice and orange peel; add 1/3 cup cocoa to flour mixture. Add 1/2 cup nonfat milk, 1 tablespoon vanilla and 1 teaspoon chocolate flavoring to oil.

Reprinted with permission from HealthMark Centers, Inc.

260

Chocolate Surprise Bundt Cake

For the chocoholic — a chocolate cake with a surprise in each bite.

Cooking spray
½ c. dried apricots, chopped
½ c. chocolate chips
½ c. walnuts, chopped
1 T. cornstarch
1 box chocolate cake mix
2 eggs
1 ½ c. low–fat buttermilk
Powdered sugar

Preheat oven to 350°. Coat a 12-cup Bundt pan with cooking spray; dust with flour. Set aside. Combine apricots, chocolate chips, walnuts and cornstarch in a small bowl; stir to coat and set aside. Combine cake mix, eggs and buttermilk in a large mixing bowl; mix at slow speed of an electric mixer until blended. Fold in apricot/nut mixture. Pour into prepared Bundt pan and bake 40–50 minutes. Cool in pan for 25 minutes, then turn out on a cooling rack. Sprinkle top with powdered sugar before serving.

Yield:
16 servings

Serving Size:
1 wedge

Preparation Time:
15–20 minutes

Cooking Time:
40–50 minutes

Nutrient Analysis per serving:

Calories: 200
Fat: 8.2 gm
Cholesterol: 23 mg
Sodium: 160 mg

Buttermilk actually contains no butter and usually has very little fat. Most buttermilk today is made from skim or low–fat milk.

Bread Pudding
with Rum Sauce

Yield:
   6 servings
Serving Size:
   4x2½-inch piece
   with 3 T. sauce
Preparation Time:
   10 minutes
Cooking Time:
   15 minutes

**Nutrient Analysis
per serving:**

Calories: 261
Fat: 3 gm
Cholesterol: 3 mg
Sodium: 248 mg

6 slices whole wheat or white bread

2 c. skim milk

1 T. margarine

4 egg whites, beaten

⅔ c. sugar

½ c. raisins

½ tsp. cinnamon

¼ tsp. nutmeg

1 tsp. vanilla

RUM SAUCE:

1 c. skim milk

2 T. brown sugar

4 tsp. cornstarch

4 tsp. dark rum

Cut bread slices into cubes. Place bread in an 8x8x2-inch baking dish; set aside. Combine milk and margarine in a glass bowl; microwave on HIGH for 3 minutes. Mix a small amount of hot milk into beaten egg whites. Pour remaining egg mixture into milk. Add sugar, raisins, cinnamon, nutmeg and vanilla; stir. Pour mixture over bread cubes. Microwave uncovered on HIGH for 7 minutes. Continue to cook 2–3 minutes if center is not firm.

Rum Sauce: Combine milk, sugar, cornstarch and rum in a glass bowl; stir well. Microwave, uncovered, on HIGH for 2–3 minutes; stirring occasionally. Serve over warm bread pudding.

*Cornstarch has twice the thickening power of flour. To prevent lumps when cooking with cornstarch, combine it with a **cold** liquid before adding it to something hot.*

Outrageous Oatmeal Cake

1 c. quick–cooking oats, uncooked
1 ½ c. boiling water
¾ c. brown sugar, packed
¾ c. sugar
½ c. margarine
1 tsp. vanilla
2 large eggs
¾ c. flour
¾ c. whole wheat flour
2 tsp. cinnamon
1 tsp. baking soda
1 c. raisins
½ c. sunflower seeds
Cooking spray
<u>TOPPING:</u>
3 T. powdered sugar
⅓ c. unsweetened coconut

Yield:
  15 servings
Serving Size:
  3x2½-inch piece
Preparation Time:
  25 minutes
Cooking Time:
  30 minutes

*Nutrient Analysis
per serving:*

Calories:	276
Fat:	10.4 gm
Cholesterol:	24 mg
Sodium:	139 mg

Preheat oven to 350°. In a small bowl, pour boiling water over oats and let stand for 20 minutes. In a separate bowl, cream together sugars, margarine and vanilla. Add eggs; beat until smooth. In another bowl, combine flours, cinnamon and baking soda. Combine oatmeal with the creamed sugar mixture. Then add flour mixture and beat well. Fold raisins and sunflower seeds into cake batter. Spread cake batter evenly into a 13x9x2-inch cake pan coated with cooking spray; bake for 30 minutes or until a wooden pick inserted into center comes out clean. Let cake cool for 10 minutes. Sprinkle powdered sugar and coconut over cake. Allow cake to cool completely before serving.

Granny Smith Apple Crisp

A tart yet sweet flavor that only a Granny Smith apple can provide.

Yield:
6 servings

Serving Size:
2/3 cup

Preparation Time:
20 minutes

Cooking Time:
25–30 minutes

Nutrient Analysis per serving:

Calories: 143
Fat: 2.7 gm
Cholesterol: 0 mg
Sodium: 27 mg

1/3 c. regular oats, uncooked

2 T. brown sugar

1 T. flour

1 T. margarine, melted

4 T. unsweetened apple juice concentrate, thawed and divided

3–4 Granny Smith apples (1 1/2 lbs.), cored and cut into 1/2-inch slices

1/2 tsp. cinnamon

1/4 tsp. nutmeg

1/2 tsp. grated lemon peel (optional)

Preheat oven to 400°. Mix oats, sugar, flour, margarine and 1 tablespoon apple juice concentrate into a small bowl; set mixture aside for topping. Place apples in large bowl. Add cinnamon, nutmeg, lemon peel and remaining 3 tablespoons apple juice concentrate; toss well. Mound apples in an 8-inch pie plate or 2–quart casserole dish; sprinkle with topping mixture. Bake 25–30 minutes or until brown.

Lemon Angels

Can you get any more simple than 2 ingredients and a 4–minute preparation time? Probably not.

Cooking spray
1 pkg. angel food cake mix
1 can (22 oz.) lemon pie filling
Chopped nuts (optional)
Shredded coconut (optional)

Preheat oven to 350°. Combine lemon pie filling and angel food cake mix. Spoon into a 13x9x2-inch baking pan coated with cooking spray. Bake 30 minutes. If desired, bars can be topped with chopped nuts or coconut before baking.

Yield:
    30 servings
Serving Size:
    3x1$\frac{1}{3}$-inch bars
Preparation Time:
    4 minutes
Cooking Time:
    30 minutes

Nutrient Analysis per serving:

Calories: 88
Fat: .7 gm
Cholesterol: 0 mg
Sodium: 96 mg

Apri–Nut Balls

If you have a microwave, these cookies are just moments away.

Yield:
2 dozen

Serving Size:
1 cookie

Preparation Time:
15 minutes

Cooking Time:
5–6 minutes

Nutrient Analysis per serving:

Calories: 51
Fat: 2 gm
Cholesterol: 7 mg
Sodium: 5 mg

¹/₂ **c. dried apricots, chopped**
¹/₂ **c. nuts, chopped**
¹/₃ **c. flaked coconut**
¹/₃ **c. sugar**
¹/₃ **c. dates, chopped**
1 egg
2 T. sugar

In a glass bowl combine all ingredients except 2 T. of sugar. Microwave, uncovered, on HIGH for 5–6 minutes or until mixture thickens enough to hold its shape. Cool completely. Form into 1-inch balls, then roll in remaining sugar.

Coconut is choles-terol–free, but like the oil that comes from it, coconut is high in saturated fat. For that reason, use it sparingly.

Banana Oatmeal Cookies

*These make for good munching
while you're jeeping in the mountains.*

1 ½ c. flour
1 c. sugar
¾ tsp. cinnamon
½ tsp. baking soda
½ tsp. salt
¼ tsp. nutmeg
¾ c. margarine
1 ¾ c. quick–cooking oats, uncooked
1 c. (2–3) mashed ripe bananas
1 egg, beaten
⅓ c. nuts, chopped
Cooking spray

Yield:
 4 dozen
Serving Size:
 1 cookie
Preparation Time:
 15 minutes
Cooking Time:
 10–12 minutes

*Nutrient Analysis
per serving:*

Calories: 78
Fat: 3.7 gm
Cholesterol: 4 mg
Sodium: 68 mg

Preheat oven to 400°. Combine flour and next 5 ingredients. Cut in margarine with a pastry blender or fork until mixture resembles coarse meal. Add oats, mashed bananas, egg and nuts; mix thoroughly. Drop by teaspoonful onto cookie sheet coated with cooking spray. Bake 10–12 minutes.

Would you choose an oatmeal cookie or a granola bar? Some commercial oatmeal cookies have half the calories and as much as 60% <u>less</u> fat than is found in some granola bars.

Snickerdoodles

A whole wheat version of a favorite holiday cookie.

Yield:
3¹/₂ dozen

Serving Size:
1 cookie

Preparation Time:
20 minutes

Cooking Time:
24–30 minutes

Nutrient Analysis per serving:

Calories: 62
Fat: 2.4 gm
Cholesterol: 4 mg
Sodium: 53 mg

1 c. sugar
¹/₂ c. margarine, softened
1 egg
2 T. skim milk
1 tsp. vanilla
1 tsp. baking powder
¹/₂ tsp. baking soda
¹/₂ tsp. nutmeg
¹/₂ tsp. salt (optional)
1 T. grated lemon or orange peel (optional)
2 c. whole wheat flour
¹/₂ tsp. cinnamon
2 T. sugar

Preheat oven to 375°. Cream 1 cup sugar and margarine together. Add egg, milk, vanilla, baking powder, baking soda, nutmeg, salt and orange peel; mix well. Stir in flour. Shape into 1-inch balls. Combine cinnamon and 2 tablespoons sugar. Roll dough balls in sugar–cinnamon mixture; place 2 inches apart on ungreased cookie sheet. Bake 8–10 minutes or until very lightly browned.

Hint: Do not overmix, it causes flat cookies.

Use shiny cookie sheets and cake pans for baking. Dark pans absorb more heat and cause baked products to overbrown.

EXCHANGE LIST

APPETIZERS & SNACKS	Bread	Meat	Vegetable	Fruit	Milk	Fat
Appetizers & Snacks: Cold						
Cajun–Style Garbanzo Nuts	1.5					
Chili Popcorn	.5					.5
Colorado Crab Spread		1.5				.5
Cool Garden Pizza	1					1
Cripple Creek Caviar	1					
Crunchy Snack Mix	1					.5
Curry Dip						
Dilly Dip						
Fresh Tomato Antipasto						.5
Herbed Deviled Eggs		.5				
Herb Yogurt Cheese Spread						
Lemon–Strawberry Punch				1		
Nutty Apricot Cheese Spread		.5		.5		.5
Peach Pizzazz Punch				2		
Salmon–Stuffed Tomatoes		.5				
Seasoned Cheese–Stuffed Tomatoes						
Spicy Corn Dip	.5					
Spinach Dip in Rye						
Strawberry Yogurt Cheese Spread						
Yogurt Cheese Spread						
Appetizers & Snacks: Hot						
Caraway Jack Potato Skins	.5					
Mexican Artichoke Dip	.5		1			
Oven–Fried Zucchini Sticks			1			
Pita Wedges with Italian Sauce	.5					
Savory Stuffed Mushrooms	.5		.5			
Stuffed Mushrooms Florentine	.5		.5			
Sweet & Sour Meatballs		1				
Teriyaki Ribbons		1				
BREADS						
Blue Ribbon Zucchini Bread	1			1		1
Cranberry Nut Bread	1			1		1
Dilly Casserole Bread	1.5					

BREADS *(con't)*	Bread	Meat	Vegetable	Fruit	Milk	Fat
Dude Ranch Whole Wheat Biscuits	1					.5
Gold Rush Carrot Bread	1					1
Harvest Pumpkin Bread	1			1		1
Honey Whole Wheat Bread	1					
Quick Yeast Rolls	1.5					
Swedish Rye Bread	2					
MUFFINS						
Fresh Raspberry Muffins	1			1		1
Honey–Lemon Muffins	1			.5		1
Make–Ahead Batter for Bran Muffins	1					.5
Mountain Biker's Banana Muffins	1			1		1
Oatmeal Blueberry Muffins	1					.5
Poppy Seed Poundcake Muffins	1			1		1
Trail Ride Zucchini Muffins	1			1		1
BRUNCH						
Backpack Muesli	2			1	.5	1
Breakfast Burritos	2	1				
Country Brunch Casserole	1.5	1.5				
Cranberry–Orange Pancakes	1.5			.5		1
Cran–Raspberry Topping				1		
Crustless Vegetable Cheese Pie		2.5	1		.5	
French Coffee Cake	1			1.5		1
Fritatta Primavera		1	1			
Fruit Kabobs and Honey Yogurt				1		
German Pancake with Saucy Apples	1			1		1
High Country Rhubarb Coffee Cake	1			1		1
Oat Bran Waffles	2					.5
Oatmeal Apple Griddle Cakes	1					.5
Oven–Baked French Toast	2	.5		.5		.5
Spicy Oat Pancakes	1					.5
Sunday Morning Scramble	.5	1.5	.5			.5
Swedish Pancakes with Cointreau Strawberries	1.5	.5		1		1.5
Turkey Sausage		1.5				
Wild Mountain Blueberry Pancakes	.5			.5		

DESSERTS (con't)	Bread	Meat	Vegetable	Fruit	Milk	Fat
Apri–Nut Balls				.5		.5
Banana Oatmeal Cookies	1					1
Bananas Grand Marnier				2		.5
Bread Pudding with Rum Sauce	1			2	.5	.5
Cherries in the Snow	1			3	1	2
Chocolate Meringue Kisses						
Chocolate Surprise Bundt Cake	1			1.5		1.5
Cranberry Cottage Cake with Lemon Sauce	1			1		1
Creative Carrot Cake	1			1		1
Easy Apple Extraordinaire				1.5		1
Fresh Apple Cake	.5			1		1
Fresh Fruit Parfait				1.5		
Frozen Pumpkin Squares	.5			2	.5	
Fruit Burritos with Chocolate Sauce	1			1		
Fruit Custard Dessert Pizza	1			2	.5	1
Granny Smith Apple Crisp				2		
Lemon Angels				1		
New–Fashioned Oatmeal Cookies	1					1
Orange Pound Cake	1					1
Outrageous Oatmeal Cake	1			2		2
Peanutty Rice Krispie Pie	1	.5		1		1
Redstone Rhubarb Crisp	1			2		1
Snickerdoodles	1					.5
Strawberry Lemon Trifle	1			?		
Western Slope Peach Melba				2	.5	
FISH & SEAFOOD						
Backyard Grilled Tuna Steaks	4					
Bay Scallops with Peppers and Pasta	1.5	1		.5		.5
Cheese–Topped Orange Roughy		3				.5
Chinese–Style Poached Fish		3				
Clam–Filled Lasagna Rolls	1.5	3.5	1		.5	1
Cucumber Dill Sauce						.5
Fettuccine with Shrimp Sauce	3	2				.5
Fish in Creamy Dill Sauce		2				
Fish Ole'		4	.5			

FISH & SEAFOOD *(con't)*	Bread	Meat	Vegetable	Fruit	Milk	Fat
Garlic Shrimp on a Bun	1	1				.5
Honey Mustard Salmon		4		1		
Italian Fish in Foil		3	1	.5		
Landlubber's Salmon Patties		3	.5			1
Lemon Grilled Trout		2				.5
Linguine with Salmon and Lemon Sauce	3	1.5				1.5
Shrimp Jambalaya	1	1	2			.5
Spicy Shrimp Boil	2.5	1.5		1		3
Steamed Halibut with Roasted Pepper Sauce		4	1			
Teriyaki Swordfish		3		.5		
Trout Almandine	1	3				1
Wine–Baked Salmon with Tarragon Sauce		4				
KIDS CUISINE						
Berry Breakfast Shake				2	1	
Chicken Nuggets	.5	2				
Cinnamon and Sugar Wonton Chips	.5					
Crowded Canoes		.5		.5		1
Crunchy Bananas				1.5		.5
Honey Hug				.5	1	
Mini Muffin Pizzas	1	1		.5		.5
Orange Smoothies				1.5		
Peanut Butter Bread	1					.5
Peanutty Chocolate Pops		1		1	.5	3
Pumpkin–Oat Pancakes	2			.5	.5	.5
Sloppy Toms	2	2.5	1			
Waffle Sundae	1	.5		1.5		1
MEATS						
Buffaloaf	.5	3				2
Cinnamon Grilled Pork Tenderloin		4				
Durango Short Ribs	1	4	1			1
Glazed London Broil		4.5				1
Krautburgers	2	1				1
Lemon Ginger Lamb Chops		3		2		
Old–Timer's Beef Stew	1	4	1.5			.5
Oriental Pepper Steak	3	3	1			.5

272

MEAT *(con't)*	Bread	Meat	Vegetable	Fruit	Milk	Fat
Pizza Burgers		4				1.5
Pork Chops in Apple Juice		3		1		.5
Rancher's Meat Loaf	.5	2				1
Royal Gorge Rack of Lamb		3				
San Luis Barbecued Beans	3	1		1		.5
Sesame Pork with Broccoli		4	2			1
Smokey Beef Brisket	.5	3				
Spicy Grilled Chops		3		.5		.5
Tremendous Tenderloin Steaks		4.5				
Vegetable Burgers	1	1.5				.5
MEXICAN						
Alamosa Posole	1		.5			
Carne Adovado		3				.5
Black Bean Tostadas	3	1	1			1
Chili Relleno Casserole	2.5	.5	1			
Cortez Chicken Enchiladas	2	3.5	1			.5
Firecracker Enchilada Casserole	2	2.5	1			.5
Five–Layer Mexican Dip	.5					
Green Chili Soup	.5	1	1			.5
Green Chili Squash	.5		1			.5
Grilled Fajitas	1.5	2				.5
Mexican Beef Stir–Fry		3	1			1
Mexican Cornbread	1	.5				.5
Mock Sangria				1		
Oven Tortilla Chips	1					
Pronto Taco Bake	1.5	2.5	.5	1		2
Salsa Fresca			1			
Santa Fe Beans	2.5		.5			
Summer Siesta Salad	1	2.5	1			.5
PASTA & GRAINS						
Alpine Rice and Mushrooms	1					.5
Berthoud Pass Bulgur	1		.5			.5
Dove Creek Anasazi Beans	1.5					.5
Garden Rice	1.5		.5			
Leadville Lasagna	1	2.5	1		.5	.5
Mexican Bulgur	1.5		.5			.5
Pasta with Fresh Tomato Sauce	3		1.5			2

PASTA & GRAINS (con't)	Bread	Meat	Vegetable	Fruit	Milk	Fat
Red Beans and Rice	3.5		1			
Savory Green Rice	1		.5			
Spicy Fruited Rice	1			.5		.5
Sweet & Sour Lentils	1.5					.5
Tabor Tabbouleh	1.5		1			.5
POULTRY						
Blackened Chicken Breasts		3				.5
Breast of Chicken Dijon		3		1		
Broccoli Cashew Chicken	.5	3	1			2
Chicken Cacciatore		3	1.5			
Chicken Curry		2	1			.5
Chicken in Orange–Almond Sauce		3		1.5		2
Grilled Chicken with White Barbeque Sauce		3				
Indonesian Chicken in Peanut Sauce	1.5	4	2			1
Mediterranean Chicken with Mushrooms	3		2.5			
Moroccan Stuffed Chicken	1	3				1
Oven–Fried Italian Chicken	1	6		1		
Rosemary Lemon Chicken		3	.5	.5		
Saucy Chicken and New Potatoes	1.5	3	.5			1.5
Sesame Ginger Chicken		3				
Sweet & Sour Chicken	1	2	1	1		.5
Tandoori Chicken		3				
Tarragon and Wine Poached Chicken		3	.5			
Turkey Piccata	1	3		.5		1
SALADS						
Breckenridge Broccoli Salad			.5	.5	.5	
Carrot–Raisin Salad with Orange Yogurt Dressing			.5	1		
Chili Cheese Salad		1	1			
Confetti Pasta Salad	1.5		.5			
Garden Pasta Salad	1		1			
Jicama and Orange Salad				1		
Miner's Corn and Kidney Bean Salad	1.5					
Ramen Slaw	1		.5			1

SALADS (con't)	Bread	Meat	Vegetable	Fruit	Milk	Fat
Saucy Fruit Salad				2		
Spinach in a Mold				1		
Supreme Spinach Salad			.5	.5	.5	1
Sweet & Sour Pasta Salad	1		.5	1		
Tempting Tortellini Salad	1					1
Warm Broccoli Potato Salad	1		1			1
MAIN DISH SALADS:						
Asparagus Salmon Salad		2	1.5			2
Broadmoor Chicken Salad		1.5	5			2
Oriental Salad		2.5	.5	.5		.5
Polynesian Chicken Salad		2	.5	.5		1
Quick Taco Salad	3	.5	1			2
Snowmass Shrimp Louis	.5	1				.5
Spinach Salad with Fruit & Beef		3	1	1		1
Tuna on a Shoestring	.5	1	1			1
SOUPS						
Boulder Black Bean Soup	1	.5				1
Broccoli–Chicken Soup	1	.5	1			
Carrot–Cashew Soup	1	.5	2			2
Chilled Cucumber–Herb Soup			.5		.5	
Creamy Potato Soup	1.5					.5
Easy Tortilla Soup	1.5	.5	1			
Glenwood Gazpacho			2			
Gringo Chili	1	2	2			
Hearty Lentil Stew	2.5		1			
Rocky Mountain Oyster Stew		1			1	1.5
Savory Seven Bean Soup	1.5	1	.5			
Skier's Vegetable Chili	2		1.5			.5
Southwestern Stew	2	3	.5			.5
Split Pea Soup, "No Hassle"	2	1	.5			
Velvet Corn Chowder	1	.5				
Winter Stew	1	1	1.5			.5
VEGETABLES						
Broccoli with Dill Cheese Sauce		.5	1			
Deli Carrots						
Garlic Squash on the Grill			1			
Green Beans Telluride			2			.5
Grilled Corn-on-the-Cob	1					

VEGETABLES *(con't)*	Bread	Meat	Vegetable	Fruit	Milk	Fat
Grilled Potato Salad	1.5		.5			.5
Ranch Potato Topper		1				
Riverside Picnic Vegetables	1		.5			1
Roaring Fork Ratatouille			1.5			
Sesame Broccoli			1			
Skillet Zucchini Pancake	.5	.5	.5			.5
Skinny Oven Fries	1					.5
Spaghetti Squash Marinara	1		1	1		1
Sweet & Sour Carrots			1	1		
Tangy Mashed Potatoes	1.5					.5
Vail Vegetable Medley			1			
VEGETARIAN						
Claim Jumper's Black Bean Stew	4.5	.5	2			.5
Confetti Couscous Casserole	5	2.5	1.5			1
Eggplant Parmesan	.5	1	2	1		1.5
LaJunta Lentil Bake	1.5	1.5	1			.5
Lean and Luscious Potato Split	1	1				.5
Lentil Spaghetti Sauce	2.5	.5	2			
Manicotti in Minutes	1.5	1	1.5	1	.5	1.5
Mesa Verde Black Beans and Rice	5		1			
Spinach Enchilada Casserole	2	1	1.5			.5
Vegetable Calzones	4	2	2	.5		1

INDEX

278

279

280

282

283

284

288

Testers, Tasters and Contributors

Rosanne Ainscough
Lesta Allen
Marlene Allen
Shannon Allen
Carolyn Andersen
Jennifer Anderson
Sherry Anderson
Debbie Andrews
Mildred Arnold
Shirley Arthur
Wendy Askelson
Janet Aumann
Connie Auran
Shirley Beth Babler
Chris Bachman
Doris Baker
Karen Baker
Judy Barbe
Alice Barber
Ann Barney
Laren Barnett
Carol Battalora
Lynn Baughman
Patty Baumgard
Kelly Beach
Rebekah Bendele
Claudia Benedict
Anne Bennett
Jackie Berning
Carol Berry
Sally & Dick Billows
Lynette Black
Becky Bledsoe
Carole Bogedain
Chris Book
Suzanne Boos
Mary Lee Bost
Ruth Bowling
Luann Boyer
Vivian Bradford
Wilma Bradley
Mary Branom
Laura Brieser
Jan Brown
Kathy Brown
Rhonda Bruns
Jennifer Bullock
Susan & Dan Bunch
Marilyn Burger
Joy Burke
Debbie Burton
Donna Buskirk
Lisa Butts
Dorothy Buxton

Phyllis Bweenheide
Eva Byron
Kay Campbell
Lori Careswell
Caroline Cassens
Jean Cassidy
Kathleen Chaffer
Cherie Chao
Tracy Chidestes
Karen Christensen
Elizabeth Ciuffini
Ada Clark
Libby Coates
Dianna Collins
Louise Collins
Velma Combers
Meg Conant
Jane Connell
Kate Connors
Shirley Conrad
Anjenette Cooper
Karen Corueil
Patricia Corwin
Wanda Cousar
Judy Cox
Shirley Craighead
Maria Creavin
Margaret Crowell
Clare Cusumano
Shelly Czopek
Patricia Daniluk
Bonnie Davis
Carole Davis
Marilyn Day
Kathy Dechtman
Liz Marr Diemand
Karin Dilger
Joan Divine
Lou Ann Dixon
Peggy Dlugos
Elizabeth Donnelly
Helen A. Dorrough
Louise Downey
Julie Dutton
Ruby Earnshaw
Claudia Ehrlich
Jenny Eikenberry
Julie Elliott
Margaret Elliott
Carol Emich
Jamie Erskine
Lisa Esch
Audeen Faller
Melanie Faught

Mark Kay Fellion
Margaret Flickinger
Beth Foley
Judy Fowler
Rosalind Fowler
Dee Fox
Janet Franz
Janet Frazier
Catherine Freeman
Lou Fritz
Rita Gee
Brenda Germann
Joyce Gibson
Kathy Glaaser
Kathryn Goetz
Becky Good
Susan Gould
Sharon Graham
Marian Griffen
Mary Halkett
Pamela Ham
Susan Hamilton
Carolyn Hammond
Karen Hanson
Jane Harrell
Carole Harris
Dawn Hasebroock
Jan Patenaude Haugen
Karen Hayes
Karen Haywood
Edith Heberlein
Henrietta Hehn
Donna Hendrick
Connie Hereford
Jane Hermanson
Shannon Herron
Sue Hicks
Beverly Hilleary
Ann Hines
Ellen Hird
Judi Hoback
Michelle Hoelting
Martha Holland
Susan Hollister
Sandra Holmes
Phyllis Holtan
Lilly Ann Huppert
Patti Infante
Cathy Jahde
Jennifer Jeary
Fran Jessup
Candace Johnson
Cindy Kalmar
Karol Kendall

Pat Kendall
Nancy Kennedy
Helene Kent
Karri Kent
Karla Klemm
Jan Kochis
Nancy Kosares
Konnie Krahn
Cindy Krisinger
Donna Krug
Vicki Krul
Linda Kwiatkowski
Merna Kybic
Sarah Harding Laidlaw
Felice Larsen
Dorothy Lauer
Sara Lemley
Kris Lenczycki
Angela L'Hereaut
Debbie Limoge
Pat Lindorff
Shirley Lippincott
Sharon Lloyd
Lyndy Lubbers
Elise Lubell
Nancy Macey
Ruth Marr
Suzanne Mason
Dean Massey
Kay Petre Massey
Mildred Masteller
Amy Mathiesen
Judy Matthews
Jean Massey
Cynthia May
Kathryn McClain
Bunny McComb
Gwen McConnell
Tracy McCune
Tami McFerren
Joan McGill
Anita McGregor
Cathie McKibbon
Bonnie Melia
Janet Mertz
Mary Lou Millbern
Carol Miller
Gale Miller
Carolyn Miner
Nancy Mohler
Sue Moore
Melinda Morris
Star Morrison
Betzi Murphy
Ginny Murphy
Lori Nelson

Susan Neuwirth
Jackie Nielsen
Jan Nixon
John Nizzi
Peggy Norton
Ann O'Neill
Cathleen Orr
Loretta Orton
Beth Pannbacker
Sidney Park
Alice Parker
Marsha Parker
Lucy Patterson
Debra Paulsen
Mary Peet
Jo Ann Pegues
Paula Peirce
Lucille Pelech
Courtney Petre
Lois Petre
Patty Petre
Lori Ann Piazza
Gianna Pierce
Sharlene Piper
Sharon Pope
Nancy Pudwill
Archie Ransom
Joy Ranum
Renee Ratcliff
Patty Reid
Elsa Reynolds
Wendy Rice
Shirley Rieke
Marcia Rinker
Doris Rohde
Jane & Jerry Robinson
Norma Robinson
Nancy Rosner
Marian Ruge
Marion Ruybal
Linda Ryan
Lucille Saso
Bonnie Sawyer
Mary Schaefer
Patti Schapiro
Kate Schiltz
Debie Schissler
Karla Schmidt
Lois Schmitt
Cynthia Scholl
Linda Schoon
Jean Schreiner
Mary Schroeder
Judy Schure
Barbara Schwartz
Bonnie Schweder

Lisa Shepard
Mary Sinkay
Rebecca Sisler
Ann Skemp
Julie Smith
Sheryl Smolik
Sandra Spence
Claire Steinberger
Yvonne Steinhour
Daniel Stern
Susan Stevens
Lynn Stevenson
Deborah Stewart
Debbie Swanson
Sally Swartz
Peg Swath
Bridget Swinney
Mary Taylor
Donelle Thomas
Helen Thompson
Myrtis Thompson
Lyn Thor
Doris Tietge
Lynn Tokach
Nancy Trebella
Pam Truesdale
Sheryl Tsuchimoto
Lillian Tu
Kristin Tucker
Terry Tusberg
Helen Utley
Carole VandeKoppel
Brenda Vrzak
Jean Wagenaar
Brenda Walter
Nena Warren–Felsher
Palmer Watson
Sharon Weiss
DeAnn Whitmire
Sandy Wickam
Crystal Widynowski
Melissa Wiles
Karen Wilken
Carolyn Williams
Mary Williams
Diane Windes
Elisabeth Wirick
Karen Wolfe
Eleanor Wong
Mary Wood
Gretchen Woodard
Gretchen Woodfield
Marianne Woodward
Melanie Wright
Lori Yenser
Clara Zerbe

Colorado Dietetic Association • 4945 Meade Street
Denver, Colorado 80221 • 303/477-6314

Name _____

Address _____

City/State/Zip _____

Please send me the indicated quantity of *Simply Colorado – Nutritious Recipes for Busy People.*

Quantity	Price Each	Colorado Sales Tax (Denver–Metro)	OR	Colorado Sales Tax (Outside Metro)	TOTAL
_____	$14.95	$1.09/book	OR	$.57/book	$_____

Plus $3.00 per book for shipping and handling $_____

                          TOTAL ENCLOSED $_____

Please make checks payable to: Colorado Dietetic Association
Please do not send cash. Sorry, no C.O.D.'s

Profits from the sale of these cookbooks are used to support the purpose
and programs of the Colorado Dietetic Association.

- -

Simply COLORADO

Colorado Dietetic Association • 4945 Meade Street
Denver, Colorado 80221 • 303/477-6314

Name _____

Address _____

City/State/Zip _____

Please send me the indicated quantity of *Simply Colorado – Nutritious Recipes for Busy People.*

Quantity	Price Each	Colorado Sales Tax (Denver–Metro)	OR	Colorado Sales Tax (Outside Metro)	TOTAL
_____	$14.95	$1.09/book	OR	$.57/book	$_____

Plus $3.00 per book for shipping and handling $_____

                          TOTAL ENCLOSED $_____

Please make checks payable to: Colorado Dietetic Association
Please do not send cash. Sorry, no C.O.D.'s

Profits from the sale of these cookbooks are used to support the purpose
and programs of the Colorado Dietetic Association.